Beyond the "After" Life

Steven Bates

STEVEN BATES

Also available from Steven Bates

Reflections of a Beret

The "After" Life

Forgotten Places

Caleuche Chronicles

Beyond the "After" Life

Copyright © 2019 by Steven Bates. All rights reserved. Published by Forgotten Places Publishing. Printed in the U.S.A. and Great Britain

1st edition

For more information see:

www.facebook.com/StevenBatesMusings

www.facebook.com/ForgottenPlacesPublishing

or

www.forgottenplacespublishing.com

Follow Steven Bates on twitter: @StevenBatesPoet

Cover Art by Victoria Cline

No part of this publication may be reproduced in whole or in part, or stored in a retrieval system, or transmitted in any form or by any means: electronic, mechanical, photocopying, recording, or otherwise, without written permission of the Publisher and Author. For information regarding permission, write to:

Forgotten Places Publishing

2200 Park Pl

Cheyenne, WY 82001

Copyright © 2019 Steven Bates All rights reserved.

ISBN: 978-1-944621-23-0

Table of Contents

Acknowledgements 9
Dedication 11
Chapter 1: A Few Random Thoughts 13
    The Human Within 14
    Voices 16
    Unshamed 18
    Awash on the Shore 22
    Sadness 26
    I Broke Our Family 28
    To Mariah 32
    End of a Chapter 34
    We Took It in Stride 36
    Death Dream 38
    I Think I Woke Up Dead Today 40
    Even Rocks Crumble 44
    Depression: Alone in the Darkness 46
    On Hope 48
    You Have Never 50
Chapter 2: Inspirations from Chaplain Delbert Hansen 53
    Saint Delbert 54
    The Man That Married Me 56
    "Good Morning Friend" 60
    My Quest for His Last 62
    Prescription for Life 68
    Why Must I? 70

After 72
Chapter 3: Honor and Patriotism 75
   The Cost of the Golden Star 76
   The Call Was Not for Me 78
   A Stitch for Time 82
   One Hundred Years 84
   In Memory 86
   Not My President 88
   At What Cost 90
   At Rest 92
   Honor 94
   All It Meant 96
   Over There a King 98
   All I Have Part 2 102
   Beret Blues 106
   The Hills Have H-Bombs 108
   His Star of Bronze 112
Chapter 4: Spiritual 115
   Drinking Away My Problems 116
   The Beginning Was Always About the End 118
   Salvation Splinters 120
   Sunrise Serenity 124
   Hollow Eyes 126
   Validation 130
   Redemption 132
Chapter 5: PTSD Ponderings 135
   "On" 136

The War Came Home	140
Struggles	142
Post-traumatic Stress Disorder	144
My Mind is MIA	148
PTSD	150
What is PTSD to Me?	152
A Moment in Time	154
Helmets and Hardships	156
MIDDLE AGE CRISIS	160
Chapter 6: Affairs of the Heart	163
True Love's Touch	164
Showered by Blessings in a Springtime of Hell	166
I Found What You Lost	168
My Soul	170
Little Treasures of Daily Life	172
Chapter 7: Lightheartedness	175
Have a Book Fair, If you Dare	176
Breaking Free	178
Contract of Fear	180
Waiting on the Cable Guy	184
Mac and Cheese	186
Adaptation	190
Scarecited	192
(with Credit to My Friend Leela)	192
Heroes	194
Waiting for It to Drop	196
50	200

Despair 202
RIP 204
Did I? 206
Chapter 8: Reflections of Nature 209
   Butterflies 210
   The Tree 212
   The Ornament 214
   Trestle to the Unknown 216
   Moonlight (an Englyn Penfyr Style Challenge Poem) 218
   Cabin by the Moonlight 220
   Two Balloons (and a Buffoon) 222
   Two Balloons 224
Chapter 9: True Stories of Real People 227
   Could I Have Been the One? (For My Uncle) 228
   Funny Colored Eyes to See 232
   Discovery 236
   The Journey Home 240
   Four Days Our Angel 242
Chapter 10: Songs and Lyrics 245
   My Truck, It's Me It Tries to Kill 246
   Did You Smell That Smoke? 250
   Still Haven't Found That Reason 254
   How I Cried for Suicide 258
   The Blur from the Bottom of the Bottle 262
   Unpacking 40 Years 266
   The Box 268
   Nail in the Coffin 272

Final Thought 277
   The Whole Story 278
About Steven Bates 282

Acknowledgements

So many people to thank, so many incidents to blame, yet so much good from the former to help survive the latter. My wife, Sandra, of course is my rock, truly my life-giver and caretaker. She has encouraged me to no end, comforted me when I was at the end, and has promised to be with me until the end. For her I am grateful and thankful for so much. This book, and an entire chapter, is dedicated to now passed away Chaplain Delbert Hanson. Chaplain Delbert was the chaplain that married my wife and I at a wonderful ceremony at Poor Richards restaurant in Cheyenne, WY. He was ill at the time yet promised he would perform the ceremony and that he did, even after wobbling to the point we had to get him a chair and he finished the wedding from a sitting position. Chaplain Delbert continued to be an inspiration and would come to me at the VA to give me an idea or one liner to start a poem with. I sat beside Chaplain Hansen in his final days at a hospice and yet, facing death, he was a fountain of positivity and would continue to feed me ideas even as he could barely talk. The poems he inspired are in this book, and I hope they inspire the reader as much as he inspired me. Another person I must acknowledge is Josh Walker, my friend and publisher. Josh has been an incredible example of what an author should be and how he should care about what his readers want. I remember the first time I spoke to Josh via phone while I was vacationing in Missouri with family. His faith in me never wavered from that phone call on and he continually has encouraged me at every turn. While we are speaking of encouragement, another person to acknowledge is the incredible voice talent of Paul Tuttle. Paul is the very talented voice on all my audio books, including this one. Paul is a Navy veteran that has also always believed in this flyboy's dream, and always given me the amazing encouragement to continue my work. Please give his work a listen, you will be mystified by the quality and talent you will hear. My parents are of course the last I will mention only because they were there from the beginning. Alpha to Omega as it were. My father and mother have always been an inspiration, always been an example in what to believe and how to act as a human being and American citizen. Both my parents, while thousands of miles away, continually support and encourage me.

STEVEN BATES

Dedication

To Chaplain Delbert Hanson, for the wisdom, faith, and spirit you gave me and everyone whoever came in contact with you.

Chapter 1: A Few Random Thoughts

STEVEN BATES

The Human Within

No matter the shine or dents in the steel
No matter the wounds that batter the will
No matter the armor that covers the skin
We must always remember the Human within
The knight that comes saves us, or the knight that we are
Is never too distant, never too far
always in armor, always feels safe
Always protected (though the armor must chafe)
But what of the human that hides in the shell?
The fragile frail body not doing so well
They must wear the armor, to hide all their doubt
Confusion, and pain, fear within and without
When may they then shed this metal tin suit?
When will the need for the armor be moot?
When is the battle with evil complete,
And the armor is shed, to fall at their feet?
When will we all get all along in this world?
When will attacks, and rocks not be hurled?
It's only not needed, it will be only when
We all can remember, the Human within

Thoughts and Reflections

STEVEN BATES

Voices

So many voices

So many tones

So many choices

So many unknowns

So how will they narrate

My words into speech?

And how will they contemplate

The thoughts I beseech?

How will I know

My meanings are clear?

And how will they show

The message I hold so dear?

For I must trust in these voices

These talents on loan

Their skills and their choices

Of inflections and tone

So I trust in the feelings

From my written word

And hope in these dealings

These voices are heard

Beyond the "After" Life

Thoughts and Reflections

STEVEN BATES

Unshamed

Since those days I tried to hide
My fateful tries of suicide
I thought that folks would mock me so
Because of times I tried to go

As I look back, I've learned to say
Depression clenched my soul at bay
It held me in its' tightest grip
And there my mind began to slip

It wasn't logic in the simplest terms
That led my mind to feed the worms
With my dead corpse, I'd finally have a cause
I'd end my life without so much a pause

But treatment came in many a form
From pills and counselors to make me "norm"
I'm still not cured, my mind still haunts
Those deep dark places with those chilling taunts

But I've learned how now to control desire
To dance too close to the "suicide fire"
Like a moth to flame I fight to live
Every bit of strength this fight I give

I stand now proud that I have survived
The attempts, the thoughts, the times I've tried
I'm here to tell you, you're not alone
When depression hits, just pick up the phone

There are people to talk to, text, or write
That are there to help you in this struggle, this fight
People who've been there, people that know
What "checking out" means, when you feel it's your time to go

Beyond the "After" Life

The most meaningful thing is that you swallow your pride
Don't be ashamed, don't cower, don't hide
Talk to someone, bend their ear, make them hear
Make them listen to you, let them know what you fear

Be unashamed of asking for aid
And talk to someone till the urges they fade
Never let pride ever stand in your way
Of seeking some help to live one more day

So be unashamed, we all have our lows
Be unashamed, sometime that's how life goes
Be unashamed, for to live's what you seek
Be unashamed, no more are you weak

Be unashamed that you once fell so deep
As to drift in that darkness of eternal sleep
So you once fell, but you are up once again
And be unashamed, for He's forgiven your sin

Be unashamed, tell the world that you live
And be unashamed, for some peace you may give
To a soul that is aching, a soul torn apart
A soul ripped asunder, a fresh broken heart

You survived to live on, and I did as well
To tell all the world that it's not worth the Hell
It's not worth the torment, the anguish, the pain
That your loved ones will feel when your memory's slain

For life is worth living, if not for them, then for you
Just keep on with hoping and making your life all anew
Keep on believing there are things you don't know
But first be unashamed, and your courage will grow

STEVEN BATES

You see, I'm not ashamed, I cried out and got aid
When suicide seemed the only way I was afraid
But I got some help, you can too if you try
So Be unashamed, you're not weak if you cry

Thoughts and Reflections

STEVEN BATES

Awash on the Shore

Alone on the beach

Of depression, despair

The waves out of reach

In the cold wintry air

Whitecaps just taunting

And teasing of hope

With larger waves daunting

Like the end of your rope

Sands shifting silent

As your thoughts while you walk

Go to sad, dark and violent

And an outline of chalk

But who'd find the remains

Of the way out that you've planned?

And who'd be there to explain

Of a corpse in the sand?

Who'd know the cause,

The rhyme or the reason,

Beyond the "After" Life

You gave your life pause
In this cold weather season?
But as you ponder these questions
There's a light on the shore
That breaks ruminations
As from a lighthouse it pours
The light, it surrounds you
And warms to your soul
Breaking up despair blue
That has taken its toll
You feel now there's hope
From the beacon so bright
That now you can cope
As you bathe in its light
Then dawn slowly breaks
And the dark fades away
As the Sunrise it takes
All your blues on this day
So let the light find you

STEVEN BATES

Whenever life's bland

Let waves of hope crash through

Your line in the sand

Let your light shine

From within and without

And know you'll be fine

Of that never doubt

Beyond the "After" Life

Thoughts and Reflections

Sadness

Fuzzy grayness fills my soul
As darkened thoughts surround me
Depression takes a heavy toll
As heart beats ever slowly
Tears flow free as pain erupts
From within my core so deep
As if my insides rip my guts
And blood from wounds does seep
Clouds grow dark in skies above
As gloom and doom defeat me
For pain so great has come from love
Which left me sad and lonely
For once true love has touched your heart
Then leaves so quick and harshly
The anguish shreds your world apart
And heartbreak tears completely

Beyond the "After" Life

Thoughts and Reflections

STEVEN BATES

I Broke Our Family

"I just broke our family
It's the 5th one in this life
I just broke our family
Lost children, home, and wife

I ruined our relationships
With all my lazy ways
I ruined our relationships
Now my life is in a daze

The guilt is overflowing now
But I can't end it all
The guilt is overflowing now
But too sad would be that call

I need to move away from here
To let this family heal
I need to move away from here
Before all hope I kill"

Beyond the "After" Life

These things I thought just this week past
On the first day of this year
These things I thought just this week past
It was that spiral down I fear

But quick my mind sought coping skills
And reached out to my wife
But quick my mind sought coping skills
And all the good that's in this life

I know there's those that care for me
No matter how low I dive
I know there's those that care for me
At home, the phone or text live

There're resources there for you and I
To keep us safe from harm
There're resources there for you and I
Just speak and raise the alarm

For no matter how you're feeling now
Don't write that final letter
For no matter how you're feeling now
I promise it will get better

I care, We care, Loved ones care
We're here to hear and listen
I care, We care, Loved ones care
It's your Life we'd all be missin'

Beyond the "After" Life

Thoughts and Reflections

To Mariah

So good to see you again my friend

With Your brightness shining through

Your face lit up with a cheerful grin

With a glow of wonder that is you

Your ring so shiny with the promise of love

The sparkle of happiness in your eyes

And soon you'll wed with Grace from above

With a bundle of joy as your prize

My gift to you is simple fare

This poem is all I can give

Wishing the best to an incredible pair

May forever in love may you live!

Beyond the "After" Life

Thoughts and Reflections

End of a Chapter

Burdens hang like heavy weights
Hooks and barbs they swing
Breaking free as I approach the gates
As if a living nagging thing
Hooks released, the pressures gone
As the threshold I go across
The burdens drops, their chapter done
The millstone and albatross.
The chores, the hardships, and the pains,
that used to tear my world apart
Have turned instead to cheerful gains
That lift my spirits and my heart
As a chapter closes with slamming gates
The worries I have known so long
Now behind the wall abates
My heart now filled with song
For chapters start and chapters end
As life spins around the Sun
And the burdens I have put to pen
Are finally said and done
So fear not when life makes you frown
And burdens hang like curtains
For every time's a chapter down
And chapters end, that's certain!

Beyond the "After" Life

Thoughts and Reflections

STEVEN BATES

We Took It in Stride

Insults, barbs, cuts, and jabs
Punking, hazing, verbal stabs
Years ago, we hurt each other
Friend to Enemy, sister to brother

Our feelings were hurt
Our senses assailed
But though lower than dirt
Our courage prevailed

We took what was given
And kept on with our livin'
For words harshly thrown
Left no marks to be shown

No blood and no bruises
No scars or contusions
Just scabs on our feelings
From all of those dealings

We took all the heartache
The offenses, we'd take
And our sleeves stayed unfrayed
From a bully's tirade

We fought back if needed
And though often unheeded,
A challenge would end
And perhaps gain a friend

So what I am saying in this memory stroll
Is that though feelings were hurt and took out a toll
But it toughened us up in Life's challenging ride
All for the fact, that we took things in stride!

Thoughts and Reflections

_____

_____

_____

_____

_____

_____

_____

_____

_____

_____

_____

_____

_____

_____

_____

_____

_____

Death Dream

So softly treads upon my dreams
The nightmares, things of fear and screams
Vanished quick as light hits my eyes
As if forgetting would win a prize

I can't recall the abhorrent frights
Which fill my sleep with chilling sights
I can't explain the sweat-soaked shirts
Which I awaken in, with breath that hurts

I only know the horror I felt
As if on my grave I prayed and knelt
And on the tombstone read an icy fact
For etched on the date, someone had hacked

The date was past, just yesterday
But meant beneath me I did lay
I felt a tremble in the soggy ground
As if in the coffin my corpse did pound

Slamming fists against the wood
Vibrations echoed to where I stood
Then through the dirt a hand did burst
Its icy touch I swore was cursed

It clenched my heel to forbid my run
And I knew my time on Earth was done
Then as sun dawned on my corpse and me
My eyes blinked twice and what did I see?

Around my bed lay wreaths and buds
With dirt in sheets and sleeping duds
A tombstone headboard behind me fell
And I know I screamed a deathly yell

So startled was I by this fearsome scene
I awoke again to sheets all clean
Satin pillow beneath my head
But in my coffin, for I was dead

Thoughts and Reflections

STEVEN BATES

I Think I Woke Up Dead Today

I think I woke up Dead today
But I'm not really sure
I think I woke up Dead today
But I was looking for a cure
To end my pain and suffering
To cease the guilt and shame
I thought that all was ending
and there'd be no more me to blame
I thought I woke up Dead today
I was hoping not to live
I think I woke up Dead today
For I had nothing left to give
But no, I woke up seeing light
Bright and shining in my eyes
In a metal bed that held me tight
With straps of leather and ties
The light I hoped was Heaven's beam
But I regret that wasn't so
So then the straps in my mind they seemed

Beyond the "After" Life

To be chains from Down Below
I thought I woke up Dead today
If only someone had listened
I thought I woke Dead today
But it's not what I was Destined
I thought I woke up Dead today
And I screamed to no avail
I thought I woke up Dead today
From my life of living Hell
Instead I woke in hope and pain
Still found among the living
And I must say I won't try that again
For Death is not Forgiving
I thought I woke up Dead today
His grasp was ever fleeting
I thought I woke up Dead today
So glad my heart's still beating
So Glad I woke Alive today
For I learned Death's not the answer
So Glad I woke alive today

STEVEN BATES

For depression is like a cancer
It can be fought, - I'm learning how
And to myself I must be true
I'm so glad I'm in the here and now
And I hope that you are too.

Beyond the "After" Life

Thoughts and Reflections

STEVEN BATES

Even Rocks Crumble

Granite hard and stony faced
I've lived my life as I've been placed
A stoic person, head held high
With marbled glaze in steely eye

Always there to bear the weight
Of the burdens that have since become my fate
To stand with shoulders squared away
Like bedrock firm in a stalwart way

Entrenched so others do not fail
Alongside me, their strength prevails
I give them hope, support, and aid
So through life's hardships they can wade

But even now my veneer has cracked
My very core, less than intact
From pressures too intense to bear
As I forgot my own self care

I let self-doubt and worry in
And contemplated the unforgiving Sin
My strength for others had taken a tumble
For I learned the hard way, even hard rocks crumble

So learn this lesson, as I relate to you
Stand strong, be strong, to thine own self be true
Take care of yourself, your mind, your all
And don't be discouraged, because sometimes…rocks fall.

Thoughts and Reflections

STEVEN BATES

Depression: Alone in the Darkness

Alone in Darkness so Foreboding

Heartbeat nags as if it's goading

With every thump to end its beating

While Silence pounds till ears are bleeding

Yet in this cave that's been created

Cries for help somehow abated

Echoes return with mantras shouted

And all complaints are firmly doubted

Tears. they fall as stalagmites rise

Upon the floor till their very size

Imprison me within the stone

Of a little Hell, I call my Own

Yet somehow, I struggle thru the day

This cave I carry in some morbid way

For within my mind this cave ensnares

My very soul, my joy, my cares.

Thoughts and Reflections

STEVEN BATES

On Hope

The great unknown is will you wake
Once you lay your head to sleep?
Will you rise and new breath you'll take
Following your slumber deep?

Will your eyes take in the dawning light
When they open in the morn?
Or will your eyelids remain shut tight
When the new day is born?

Even though your fate's unknown
Will you turn the alarm clock on?
Will you set it to an abrasive tone
To wake you in the dawn?

That simple switch for sleep to end
It is faith in the unknown chances
I'm here to say you have Hope, my friend
No matter what your belief is

So always know before you bed
That your faith is strong, unbending
You've Hope already inside your head
That your sleep indeed will be ending

Thoughts and Reflections

STEVEN BATES

You Have Never

You've never heard me cry at night
You've never seen me weep
I spare you from the tragic sight
And hide while soft you sleep
You've never known how deep my fears
Affect the sleep I get
And you'll never get to dry my tears
Of that, I'll surely bet
You've never known I stay awake
Because I fear to sleep
And that someday my dreams will take
All that I wish to keep
I fear my hands will not be mine
Some night in wretched dreams
And try to take your life divine
While my mind sees violent scenes
No you have never known this side of me
With fear of nightmares coming true
And you have never known my agony
And I pray you never do

Beyond the "After" Life

Thoughts and Reflections

Chapter 2: Inspirations from Chaplain Delbert Hansen

STEVEN BATES

Saint Delbert

One of the most Christ-like men that I've ever known

Now sits in Heaven beside a huge golden throne

To the right-hand side where he's always been

As a servant of God to the creation called men

He walked among us all as faithful could be

An example for others just from what we could see

But deep in his heart where some knew him the best

He shone like a beacon, far out glowing the rest

He smiled when he listened, his eyes sparkled so

His depth and humanity gave a warm inner glow

He greeted with hugs, a firm handshake too

As warm as the feeling that he always gave you

His humor would brighten even my darkest day

Keeping all of my demons and devils at bay

The Spirit was filled in this Saint of a man

And I'll continue to honor him any way that I can

I miss him immensely, but I know that he's near

For with all that he taught me, I've nothing to fear

He showed us the way that we all need to love

And I'm thankful I met him, this Saint from above

Thoughts and Reflections

STEVEN BATES

The Man That Married Me

A smaller man, yet a little bit stout
I'd had no idea just he was all about
I met him while seeking a chaplain you see
In hopes that one could marry my fiancée and me

He said that he would on condition or two
He'd marry us both once the fat we would chew
We'd have to sit down and have a long talk
Before the aisle he'd allow my fiancé to walk

So we got to know the man that he was
A man of the cloth and very true to the cause
He was very committed, and as soon we found out
He'd never give up even with illness about

The day of day our wedding, he was a very sick man
But he showed up to wed us according to plan
Halfway through the vows, he developed a frown
And we rushed forward to grab him as Delbert went down

Beyond the "After" Life

But our Chaplain was stoic once we got him a chair
He pressed on like a champ with nary a care
The wedding went on, we each gave our oath
Though he sat thru the rest, he married us both p

I admired the man, his faith, and his style
And friends we became, the kind that lasts quite a while
I've learned much from Delbert, his wisdom is vast
A scholarly man, with a many storied past

I've come to think of him as my muse
He's given me so much knowledge to use
He'd walk up to me and simply amaze
By giving a title, a word, or a phrase

He'd tell me to use them, these words he would give
And I'd create poems, try to make his words live
And somehow it seemed all the poems I would write
Became solid gold with scores of hits overnight

STEVEN BATES

I can't say enough of the good this man does

For the veterans he cares for, the people he loves

Yes, surely, I'll miss seeing him walking these halls

But to Delbert, I salute you, and you earned my applause.

Thoughts and Reflections

STEVEN BATES

"Good Morning Friend"

First thing in the morning as they open the blinds
I watch the same birds gather as the sun gently unwinds
The red tipped robin, a favorite of mine
On the feeder perches, the left side is thine
A huge dove flutters its large wings to scare
The other small birds that take to the air
But the red tipped Robin, he holds to his place
For the big fat dove is his own saving Grace
The Robin knows when his dear friend is near
There are no other threats, and nothing to fear
While the huge size is scary and threatening to most
The Robin finds comfort and strength from his post
And when the Robin is full, his belly is sated
He lets out a chirping to let all know he's elated
For all was provided, he needed not worry
He needed not anger, nor wrath or such fury
For the seed's always present, the big Dove is too
His comfort, security, to all that claim knew
The Big Dove, our Father, providing all that need
From protecting from vagrants and guarding our seed
So when this life is over, we'll fly off to see
The wonder he gives us, the gift of eternity

Thoughts and Reflections

STEVEN BATES

My Quest for His Last

He laid in the VA, collapsed, reposed
His body connected, IV'ed, and hosed
Electrified, monitored, respirators on
It wasn't much time before his will was gone

He raised up his finger, barely a twitch
Was it gesture or reflex, I couldn't tell which
His eyes followed the lift with a watery plea
I felt there something he begged to tell me

I leaned forward, my ear to his lips
His hands reached for my arm with cold icy grips
His voice, for weeks unused, now croaked alive
And he whispered these words that ignited my drive

"My sons have hated me for all of their lives,
Through all of my marriages, all of my wives.
See, I left their mother when they were quite young
From that point on neither one was called son

She filled them with hatred, destroyed my gifts.
Demanded more money, created huge rifts
I went to go see them at age two and three
And I'm sorry to say that's the last they saw of me

I could've, I should've, If I'd been a better man
Tried harder to see them, to make a strong stand
Explain just what happened, why I had to leave
But then tragedy struck and caused them to grieve

Their mother, still young, died tragic at home
No chance of goodbyes, no warnings to bemoan
Her passing brought pain and tortured their souls
And I wasn't there to fill the void's darkest holes

Beyond the "After" Life

So now that I'm passing, I must make amends
And show to my sons that their hatred has ends
I must say I'm sorry from a voice not my own
And if you'll echo my feelings, my soul could be known"

I promised the old man I'd search for his kin
But with work, school, and family, I had no clue when.
Then slowly his face took on a morbid, sad state
As he resigned to the fact his request had to wait

He sucked in a breath, rather large, filled his cheek
Blew it out slowly, and in a voice soft and meek
"Isn't there some way they could know 'fore I die?
Is there ever a chance for me you could try?"

I swallowed a gulp, I promised that old man
I will do all I could, make every effort I can
To find his two boys, relay his regrets
Tell them he's sorry, ease all his frets

So I went home that night, and packed for a trip
Kissed goodbye to my wife, while off to sleep she would slip
Started my car, pulled out of the drive
Wondering just now if the old man's still alive

I drove to his eldest, quite simple it was
He'd no reason to hide from his father for cause.
He had a young wife, a daughter of two
Introducing myself, I stated "How do you do?"

"I'm not here to cause drama", but I could see in his eyes
These words from his Father came at no big surprise.
"Of course, he's repentant, of course he feels blame.
Of course, he sent you to beg pity on his shame."

"I don't need apologies, I don't need his guilt.

STEVEN BATES

I made it just fine without him or his ilk"
But as I listened intently to this young adult son
I thought of the veterans his dad lay dying among

So I stopped the young man in middle of his rant
And brought him to speed on his Father's death can't
I told of the sorrow, of his wish to make peace
Before his frail body would give up its lease

He stopped for a moment, emotions in place
Then choked back a comment as a tear hit his face
"Is he really dying? Is this really his end?
Is his Life truly over and you're his last hope of a friend?"

I described the deathbed, the VA, my Quest
How I promised their Father I would give it my best
He smiled ever weakly then held out his hand
Thanked me for coming, shook firm like a man

His eyes teared up slightly as I spoke well of his Dad
Of the lives that he's touched, the adventures he's had.
He stopped me mid-sentence as I bid him goodbye
And told me these words after a long awkward sigh

"I don't think I'll ever forget what he's done,
But tell him I love him and am proud I'm his son"
You've done him this service, this Quest like no other
I thank you for me, my mother, my Brother. "

I'll pass on your message to my Dad's other son
And grant you completion of a Quest you've well done
Now go, tell my Father that all is absolved
That his Last Request caused my heart to evolve

I know that he meant to always stay in our lives
And that I constantly blamed him for his many wives

Beyond the "After" Life

He may not have been here, but he did pay support
Even though it was ordered and required by court

He wasn't a deadbeat, he paid what he owed
But according to Mother, he was worse than a toad
I know now she hurt, felt pain from his leaving
But now I've since learned some of her 'truths' were deceiving

I've come now to peace with my mother and dad
Now that I've heard both the stories they've had
I forgive both of them of whatever reason or fault
That caused the actions of their feelings to halt

And you may now return to the man I now call my Dad
Inform your Quest is completed, my Sir Galahad
Your honor intact, your mission complete
For he may now leave this world to stand at God's feet

I got in my car, slowly turning the key
Thought to myself, what did I just now see?
A Father's great sorrow, his son's pardoning
Of the guilt and the burden he been carrying

I returned to the hospital, went straight to his bed
But found that the father was elsewhere instead
It seems once I left, he had smiled once more
And passed to the next life as I walked out the door

He knew that my mission, my Quest I'd fulfill
And forgiveness he'd have if by only sheer will
So I stopped by to see him at the grave where he lay
And I thanked him for the lesson I learned on that day

The lesson was simple, don't wait till the end
Don't hope that your sorrows are on the quest of a friend
For the chance may not come that your hopes will be heard

STEVEN BATES

And forgiveness will happen from a solemn sworn word

Seek out those you've wronged, or you think you've offended
Make sure any grievance or feuding has ended
Rest on your deathbed without fear or regret
And go your Maker with a soul clear of debt

Then I thought of the ultimate Last Request that I knew
Was "Father, forgive them, for they know not what they do"
And I know should I ever be asked once more for such quest
I will give my it my all, for He gave us His best

Beyond the "After" Life

Thoughts and Reflections

STEVEN BATES

Prescription for Life

The Chaplain that married me and my wife
Gave to me the prescription for life
It's not a pill or drug he said
But an airport location tag stamp instead
For imagine the airport in Dallas Fort Worth
Its terminal takes you all over this Earth
The three-letter code for this traveler's Mecca
Such a simple 'breviation for Life's own trifecta
You see D is for Dios, Spanish for God
Leave him on top and He'll give you the nod
Then F is for family, next in the line
Keep them in your heart and you'll be doing just fine
Next is the W, for the World is below
Keep it last in your heart and far you will go
Now imagine these three as neatly stacked spheres
The singular God, your family, world full of fears
The higher the sphere, the fewer problems there are
Till alone at the top, just you and the Star
Then as you go down, the spheres', they get bigger
Till of course the world is so huge, now doesn't' that figure?
And the World slowly rotates as though in real life
It's slowly revolving from turmoil and strife
Imagine that world spinning. trying to climb
To the top of your spheres, to be first in your line
Just remember the World, heavy and round
Will crush all the others, your life it will pound
So keep it below, and your family above
And highest of all, give God all your love
So travel the world from the airport you'll start
And keep Dallas Fort Worth as your mantra to heart

Beyond the "After" Life

Thoughts and Reflections

STEVEN BATES

Why Must I?

I just said a prayer for one who had passed
That had no gold, nor wealth was amassed
No status, friends, no current, past wives
He fed himself lately by dumpster dives
He treated all with much disdain
But yet I sang for him a joyous refrain
Though I knew not where his soul went to
I shed a tear, for this I knew
At one time past this man had said
He'd give his life for mine instead
He swore an oath for his flag to serve
When his Nation called, he'd not lost the nerve
He fought the evil, he faced our foes
As to his motives, only Heaven knows
But he signed the form, he raised his hand
And for that reason, it's here I stand
So why must I shed for this man a tear?
To repay him for his service held dear
Why Must I, even though he had changed?
It's for what he did in his past, in a life so estranged
And though this life may have passed him by
He served our dear nation and deserves a good cry.

Beyond the "After" Life

Thoughts and Reflections

After

After the heartaches, after the pains
After the leeches from life have you drained
After the storms, and after the rains
After the lessons of life have you trained

After a lifetime of doubt leaves you jaded
After a shattering of dreams that you made
After all hope of surviving has faded
After the foundation of lies have been laid

After your hand of cards have been played
After the backstabbing and being betrayed
After the assassin has inserted the blade
After your losses have gotten you frayed

After you're ready to begin all anew
After you've decided your old life is through
After that moment, after facing that fact
Then by all means change, start now and react!

Beyond the "After" Life

Thoughts and Reflections

STEVEN BATES

Chapter 3: Honor and Patriotism

STEVEN BATES

The Cost of the Golden Star

The cost one paid for this star of Gold
Cannot be traded, given or sold
The cost the burden, is a price too high
For it means a warrior has touched the sky

The stars shine brighter up above
When a gold star warrior sheds its love
The Heavens dim as if to say
Welcome home, no harm comes this way

The angels bow in humble praise
Of the gold star warrior whose life he lays
At the foot, of the Throne of God
Whom He looks down with a single nod

Gently giving the deserving soul
A welcome home where to console
The grieving family left behind
And to give to them their piece of mind

For though they mourn an empty bed
Where once their Star lay down its head
With pride they hold their head up high
To know that freedoms didn't die

Because a Star lay down a life
Oppression ended, fear and strife
No longer torment weary hearts
That's what sets those Stars apart

Yes, Freedoms stayed, and flags still fly
For a Star's Greatest Gift was to sanctify
His soul, his heart, his inner Shine
So we may live, your life and mine.

Thoughts and Reflections

STEVEN BATES

The Call Was Not for Me
(Dedicated to the Vegas Victims)

The call was not for me this time
Though the bells rang loud and clear
The call was not for me this time
Though they clanged for someone dear

The call was not for me this time
Though I wish it were instead
The call was not for me this time
For my love's among the dead

The call was not for me this time
Though so many chimes were rung
The call was not for me this time
From a lunatic with a gun

The call was not for me this time
Though I tried to shield so many
The call was not for me this time
But the Vegas odds were ag'n me

The call was not for me this time

Beyond the "After" Life

Though my duty is to answer
The call was not for me this time
But my job's to stop that cancer

The call was not for me this time
My goal to stop the madman
The call was not for me this time
The ground his twisted badland

The call was not for me this time
Yet people answered with their lives
The call was not for me this time
Husbands, brothers, children, wives

The call was not for me this time
I had a duty to protect
The call was not for me this time
Their fears found no neglect

The call was not for me this time
Or perhaps it could have been
The call was not for me this time
I just wasn't giving in

STEVEN BATES

The call was not for me this time
So when bullets hit I scoff
The call was not for me this time
Oh wait, my ringer's off

The call had been for me this time
But I saved all I could save
The call had been for me this time
And I'll answer just as brave

Beyond the "After" Life

Thoughts and Reflections

A Stitch for Time

Two hundred fifty years or so
A woman we all came to know
Took up her needle, gathered thread
And stitched together blue, white and red

She had not had the job originally
It came to her by chance you see
But she took the task with determination
To make a flag for a non-existing nation

She formed a star with five points to shine
In a field of blue would thirteen entwine
To represent the colonies new
Of a nation formed for me and you

Stripes of red, and stripes of white
She'd sewn them all for forty a' night
For forty days she sewed because
So dedicated to the flag she was

It's not told, nor has it been said
how much she pained or if she bled
but what is known is as much as lost
of the great unknown named Betsy Ross.

Thoughts and Reflections

One Hundred Years

The bells will ring this Veterans' Day
Announcing peace that came our way
The eleventh day at the eleventh hour
To prove that evil lost its power
One hundred years ago did end
The War to End All Wars, and send
A message to all the World we knew
America, the Red, White, and Blue
Defended freedom, though lost brave souls.
And even with those heavy tolls
Our Nation rose, defeating foes
That held other countries in the throes
Of evil, hatred, domination
And called for help from our Great Nation
A century now has come and gone
Since on this day an Armistice was won
So Ring those bells, and thank those vets
That we honor till the sun it sets
On the western shores of our great land
Thank All Veterans, and shake their hand
Salute the ones that fought so brave
For one hundred years our land to save.

Beyond the "After" Life

Thoughts and Reflections

STEVEN BATES

In Memory

As names are called and Taps is played
As dirt is tossed and wreaths are laid
As rifles fire, their shots salute
A flag is folded in silence, mute
Reverence given to those who passed
In battles, wars or old age at last
They left behind a legacy
To friends, companions, family
They served their country, God and flag
In hopes that freedoms never lag
They served in ways few can relate
To rid the world of evil hate
They served with bravery, proud and strong
In foreign countries, short tours and long
They served in war, they served in peace
And finally now their wars did cease
Wars with foes, illness, and strife
We thank them all, each and every life
So as we bow our heads in prayer
Remembering the lives they had to share
With family, friends, and a grateful nation
We salute them all with this Dedication

Beyond the "After" Life

Thoughts and Reflections

STEVEN BATES

Not My President

'Not my president' would seem
to be the mantra of the leftist regime
While protesting in traffic and riots in streets
There seems no end to the violence it breeds

Though to be fair, the right wing did claim
That Obama's birth was fully to blame
He wasn't a citizen of this nation so great
And it seemed his 'Change' led more into hate

Both sides disliked the president they had
But this hatred of Trump just brings out the bad
Irrational fear mongering, intolerable hate
Much more than Obama while he was Head of State

It seems that our nation divided might fall
Unless we all get together to answer the call
United once again, setting aside all our doubt
For it's shameful to me that our nation lost all Her clout

Let's all work together, not acting like brats
And respect who won the election by accepting the facts
Give Trump a chance, he is your President too
No matter the hatred or vile some spew

I'll give him a chance like Obama I gave
Please you do the same so this country we save.

Thoughts and Reflections

STEVEN BATES

At What Cost

What Cost is Freedom
What price needs paid
When lives at the altar
Of Peace have been laid

What value is life
To ensure no more war
What payment is needed
to even the score

At what point is too much
And enough is enough
What point is the cost
Too demanding, too rough

What more can you ask
Than to lay down a life
When the body count rises
Is it worth all the strife

I say to you this
When lives have been lost
That the freedoms we share
Are well worth the cost

So treasure your freedoms
Let none slip away
For the cost has been paid
And continues each day

Our brave men and women
Have spilt blood in remittance
They have in fact
Paid all of the penance

They've given their all
At their nation's behest
At what cost I ask
Just only our best

Beyond the "After" Life

Thoughts and Reflections

At Rest

The flag has been folded
The bugle's been played
A picture from Basic
By a wreath is displayed
Twenty-one guns
Gave a final salute
As the coffin is lowered
And observers stand mute
Handfuls of dirt
By family and friend
Are thrown with respect
To honor the end
A life served this country
No matter the cost
And freedom was won
But another life lost
Selfless, Courageous
Were in a eulogy said
When the Brave and Distinguished
Spoke well of the dead
The honors were given
On this sad, solemn day
For one less soul
To send into the fray
The passed knows now peace
And from Heaven is blessed
For their duty is done
And they're finally…At Rest.

Beyond the "After" Life

Thoughts and Reflections

STEVEN BATES

Honor

The job's been done, the price's been paid
The honor and respect has by the curb been laid
Long since the return of troops it was due
For faithful service and for blood spilled too
For sleepless nights, for horrific dreams
For anguish causing the endless screams
For pain and suffering no one knows
'cept those that fight with similar foes
There are those that received the praise and parades
But just as many missed on their accolades
Americans spit with mouths frothing foam
Called the vets names as they returned home
Never once welcomed by the nation they left
The honor they earned was by their homeland bereft
The veterans who fought on land not their own
For democracy battled, for freedoms alone
Not for wealth nor fame nor gain did they fight
Not for pride, just simply because it was right
So give them respect and give honor to those
Who bravely fought on, against our nation's foes
Yes, honor should be given, it's what they deserve
It's what they have earned when in Armed Forces they served
Treat them as though they had fought for your life
Honor, respect them, acknowledge their strife
Their missions are over, their debt has been paid
So give them full honors when in coffins they're laid
Stand in awe of the person and the flag draped lid
And thank God that they served in the manner they did.

Beyond the "After" Life

Thoughts and Reflections

All It Meant

Tightly packed in on a bus
Felt like cattle, all of us
Unloaded promptly, stood in file
Toe this mark! Now! Run this mile!
Wait for mealtimes, feed your face!
Every mouthful gulped at hurried pace
March to classes, March to chapel
Learn hand to hand, learn to grapple
Learn history, ethics, weapons, rules
The hardest classes, technical schools
Graduate these, then find a base
But always learning is the case
Earn your stripes, achieve some pay
All to end retirement day
A Veteran now you call yourself
And set your flag upon a shelf
But's let's reflect, as now's the time
In your Golden Years sublime
What did it mean, this life you led?
The painful journey, the blood you bled?
All it meant to me, to you
Was that your blood bled Red, White, and Blue!

Beyond the "After" Life

Thoughts and Reflections

STEVEN BATES

Over There a King

Over there I was a king

I wanted not for anything

The children screamed when I walked by

Ran out outside to see "that guy"

I brought them chocolate, brought them sweets

I brought things they considered treats

They'd come running down the dirt packed street

Gathering like spokes around my feet

I felt so proud of the job I did

Providing freedom for every kid

We'd build their schools in hopes they'd learn

So Democracy is what they'd yearn

Everywhere we'd find oppressed

Those downtrodden, with rights repressed

The kids would treat us all like kings

And try to give us simple things

Things they valued, things they held dear

Things they'd saved for through all the year

Just to know it brought a smile

To heroes ending their exile

But then there'd come that fateful day

Beyond the "After" Life

We'd rotate out from our 6-month stay

Home we'd head, each a king and hero

Then we'd land on a tarmac to become a zero

We suddenly found we'd wait in lines

For VA help with our troubled minds

The military, the public, the media left

Declared we're broken, our senses bereft

But though we helped oppressed and trodden down,

We found public opinion had stripped off our crown

Our jewels replaced with thorns of distrust

From exposure to fighting a war in the dust

PTSD, yes, though it affects every one

From seeing the carnage, the enemy has done

It's not all that we are, not all we've become

We're still somebody's father, still somebody's son

We still hold our heads high, no shame do we bear

From doing our mission, in lands over there

From treatment like Kings, though targets ourselves

Done not for the glory, medals, whistles or bells

We did as were ordered and became others' salvation

Not for the praise, applause, adulation

But as those with a mission to rescue a nation

STEVEN BATES

We gave with our lives, with unexpected coronation

Kings over there, and Heroes to the youth

We returned back home, and were considered uncouth

Unfettered animals, a ticking time bomb

Zeros and losers from the places we've come

But don't write us off, don't condemn all our lot

Please re-examine this reputation that we've all got

Know that with treatment, with medical care

We'll once more be Kings, heads held high in the air

Beyond the "After" Life

Thoughts and Reflections

STEVEN BATES

All I Have Part 2

When on that day you raised your hand

To defend with pride our own homeland

A new recruit the Army had gained

And off you went to be highly trained

Alone in the night I thought of you

All the things you'll learn to do

Exercising, Marching in green

Places to go that you've never seen

More classes, more training, more lessons you learned

Completing your Basic with Honors well earned

Standing by so proudly as you earned your beret

Then Specialty School took you later that day

Till came that one day when you stood before me

I barely had admired the person you'd come to be

In crisp uniform and new rank on your sleeve

When your phone went off and you had to leave

Beyond the "After" Life

The Nation was calling, the world was at war

For some arrogant despot had gotten quite sore

At America's greatness and what his country lacked

Just like that you were gone, not known when you'd be back

The Goal, to remove him to stand trial for his actions

Yet he booby trapped his home to protect him from factions

Of the very same people you had come here to free

Then you tripped over a wire you just couldn't see

You and an elite team that went into his palace

Couldn't have known that he held so much malice

Realizing too late it was a deathtrap in spades

The bomb ended your calling, as your light slowly fades

A folded cloth of red, white and blue,

is all I have left, to hold of you.

Our nation mourned the day you died,

but they'll never know how much I cried.

As a man I stood there, stoic and proud

as your heroics they spoke of. in a voice so loud

But then they handed me that folded cloth,

as the guns went off, I stifled a cough

I held my tears till that night in bed,

as I lay that flag where you had laid your head.

I clutched it tight against my chest

the pain from losing you my final test.

My love for you will forever remain,

as I clutch that folded cloth again.

Beyond the "After" Life

Thoughts and Reflections

STEVEN BATES

Beret Blues

Earned through sweat and painful work
Earned thru lessons I dared not shirk
Earned through crawling deep in mud
Earned through tears, pain, and blood

Worn proud perched high, my whole life long
Worn proud while marching, singing a song
Worn proud saluting at a base's gate
Worn proud defending from those filled with hate

Switched for Kevlar when combat came
Switched for Kevlar, I'll never be the same
Switched for Kevlar though deep inside
Switched for Kevlar, still a Beret with pride

Back on again when dressed in Blues
Back on again to pay my dues
Back on to lay coins upon the stone
Back on for Berets not coming home

Still worn with pride, from the very start
Still worn with pride, though in my heart
Still worn with pride, because I can say
I'm proud to be a Blue Beret

Thoughts and Reflections

STEVEN BATES

The Hills Have H-Bombs

Rows and rows of hill-like mounds

Adorn the once swamped Cajun land

Inside are payloads shaped like rounds

For nations acting out of hand

Alone they'll sit in earthen mounds

With locks and doors protecting

For peace thru power knows no bounds

Their presence, ever affecting

Serene and green, these grassy knolls

Keep safe these bullets of death

Before world events can take their tolls

And all hold a collective breath

Beyond the "After" Life

For when tempers flare and evil's on the rise

These bullets are matched to missile's end

And launched into the yonder skies

To the enemy is where we'll send

Guided through air these casings fly

To wherever a threat's imposing

Peace through Strength, it does imply

When evil despots need deposing

Then back to those hills when peace returns

Go the unspent shells of death innate

To sit dormant till the world it learns

That peace is the final mandate

STEVEN BATES

So stand I guard at these little hills

Where the payloads come and go

A thankless job that seeks no thrills

And the world need never know

How close they came to witness fire

And brimstone, sulfur, ash

For all too easy to raise the ire

When nations come to clash

Peace our mission, power our might

For tucked in those little hills

Stand ever ready for the fight

Bombs that give my nightmares chills

Beyond the "After" Life

Thoughts and Reflections

STEVEN BATES

His Star of Bronze

I once met a man way more cool than the Fonz
As he told me the story of his own Star of Bronze
He fought for his country, he bled for our flag
He dodged many bullets for that high-flying rag

Now he sings thru his pain, he shares with his song
Just wanting the world to all get along
His talent, emotions, a message they send
His songs will surprise you as your heartstrings they rend

His Bronze Star shines bright in his twinkling eyes
The pain that he suffered, his new passion belies
I feel all the fear, the sweat that he bore
My respects to this man for the Star that he wore

A young lady now wears a pin of his Star
Her eyes sparkling bright as it reflects from afar
From her lapel of her dress his star catches all light
The bronze glowing metal memories of long-ago fight

She wore his Star in the presence of many
At the Grammy awards, the irony uncanny
That this tiny Bronze Star on her chest shone more bright
Than all the stars gathered to be there that night

I am so glad I met this humble new friend
I value his mentoring as he shares to no end
His songs touch my heart, his pain fills my soul
His dull Star of Bronze just a piece of the whole

Thoughts and Reflections

STEVEN BATES

Chapter 4: Spiritual

STEVEN BATES

Drinking Away My Problems

Trips to the bars for my problems to lose
Three times a week drowning sorrows in booze
The problems still stay like rehashing old news
It's just a fact of this life, like paying your dues

Dreams and nightmares my nights do take
With innocent sounds that give me a shake
I wake to a thirst that water can't slake
And turn to a drink of the brewer's make

Children screaming, chaos allowed
Raucous commotions, noises too loud
Panic and fear within a crowd
My constant fate to which I have bowed

When I return home, I seek my escape
Into a bottle housing Superman's cape
It gives me strength and my fears abate
But solves no problems, just prolongs my fate

Problems are here, and here to stay
They can't be drank or drugged away
They must be faced, it's the only way
To keep the problems of life at bay

Now coping skills and therapies
I've found are ways my life to seize
To take good care of my problems with ease
And by giving control while on my knees

I bow down now to only one God
Give him my problems, pray for His nod
With which He will heal my troubled old bod'
His mercy and kindness, my transgressions absolved

Beyond the "After" Life

Thoughts and Reflections

STEVEN BATES

The Beginning Was Always About the End

The beginning was always about the end
For what message the beginning, did it send?
A hope, a dream, a promise made
From God to Man, the card was played
He dealt us all the winning hand
And gave to us the Promised Land
For now He sent His son to us
A baby child He did entrust
For Man to listen and Man to hear
To teach His children what not to fear
For this child He sent to a stable born
Whose death would rend the curtain torn
Would be called Jesus, Son of God
And give mankind the greatest nod
For when He grew to be a man
He spoke of Heaven, and God's own plan
To bring His children and all those who take
God in their hearts and sin forsake
But some had hate filled in their soul
And made His death their only goal
They took this man, God's only son,
Made carry a cross he was hung upon
But remember the beginning, a manger birth
Was the promise to Man who lived on Earth
And though He died, Man grieved no loss
For even at the manger, It was always the cross.

Thoughts and Reflections

STEVEN BATES

Salvation Splinters

I felt the other part of me

Lashed and tied to make a tree

Dragged on shoulders cross the plaza

On a path they call The Via Dolorosa

Scratched and dropped on rock hard stone

While jeering onlookers mocked He alone

This man beneath who carried me

My weight so much He took a knee

His crown of thorns shed blood upon

The stony timbers they had tied Him on

This man was taken to the place of Skull

Devoid of Life, its purpose null

There I watched the men in steel

Dig a hole for me upon this hill

They tied this man with tight sinews

Placed a sign reading "King of Jews"

Then came the part that I give in detail

For they held out his hands and drove in a nail

My wood cried out as this man yelled

As flesh and bone and wood impaled

But as my splinters flew away with force

Beyond the "After" Life

I felt His Blood within me course

What was driven in like pounding rain

Now calmed my spirit, eased my pain

The fluid seeped between my grains

As it was hammered in with grim disdain

The armored men then raised from land

This man attached at feet and hand

They lifted me high as He hung on

And said these words" they know not what they've done"

And to my left, and to my right

There I beheld a tragic sight

Two friends of mine, once green with moss

Had both been formed into a cross

Hung upon them each were thieves

"Forgive me" cried out one of these

And "save yourself" in a mocking tone

Cried out the other then died alone

For one had passed as a newly saved soul

The other who mocked, Hell became his goal

But as the deep, dark fluid from Him bled

And filled my splinters with Life instead

I knew this man they had hung on me

STEVEN BATES

Had given His Life on my humble tree

He could have risen from that cross

And let human life suffer tragic loss

But since He died for me and you

My splinters live, and you will too!

Beyond the "After" Life

Thoughts and Reflections

STEVEN BATES

Sunrise Serenity

Easter dawn, the reddish hues
Serenely burn the Cirrus fuse
Lighting tendrils of the clouds
While still beneath the darkness shrouds
A battlefield, a deathly grave
Where but a few last men did save
Their dying friends, the enemies' men
So they could return to fight again
But of the bodies this Easter morn
On this dusty field, a crop war torn
No man arose from where he lay
To stand defiant to death's third day
No Angels rested on the stones
To proudly claim there were no bones
No weeping Mary came to find
Her cherished Savior left cloth behind
Instead this field, unlike the Cross
Showed all the evil, and the love we've lost
And as Dawn's light streams out across
Machines of death clear morning frost
Yes, the sky lights up this Easter morn
As the Sun reigns down this land forlorn
But no hymns of praise, no Easter eggs
No sunrise service, though this land it begs
For the cleansing love that came this hour
When from the tomb He escaped Death's power
He rose, but though He died for sins
Humanity still fights to see who wins
A piece of land, an artifact
A proposal to a vote or tract
So let us all be mindful friends
Of those for whom this Easter ends
And keep the faith for He did rise
As sure as Easter Sun sets in the skies

Beyond the "After" Life

Thoughts and Reflections

STEVEN BATES

Hollow Eyes

Haunted eyes locked from across the room

Hollow and shadowed with a pretense of doom

Above a somber face they seemed to loom

As they approached me, I could feel the gloom

She looked at me, her soul to bare

Those hollow eyes, they seemed to share

All her pain, her grief, her lack of care

Reflecting in that thousand-yard stare

Her eyes, they screamed in silent fear

And though she stood just inches near

Her pupil's gaze went deep and clear

Miles into me and my soul did tear

Her voice crackled when finally, she spoke

Which wrenched my guts as my heart, it broke

She told of the horror, the loss in her life

As she had tragically lost her title of wife

Beyond the "After" Life

Her children's father, her husband of years
Had spun out of control while shifting his gears
The ice claimed its victim as he lost all control
And the impact of the wreck had paid Charron His toll

His features disfigured, a closed casket was needed
The poor children's prayers to see papa unheeded
They understood not why Dad was away
And why Mom in the bedroom crying did stay

So as mother told all, in her cracked voice I heard
All the anger and agony her loss had incurred
But then she stopped cold, her voice gained timbre
And to this very day, I'll always remember

She said very firmly with a definite nod
It was all the will of her savior, the will of her God
Her faith caught me off guard, for I wasn't expecting
The amount of true worship and sincere genuflecting

Then those haunted eyes brightened and lit from within

The hollow look faded as she lifted her chin

She stated her children, the only link to their Dad,

Had finally accepted the new life they had

Yes, their father was gone but never forgotten

And his essence lives on in the sons he'd begotten

But now a new Father from heaven beside him

Looks down on the mother and children to guide them

This new Father won't leave nor die per her fears

He won't ever give up or give cause for more tears

For He loves all His children, saving even those Lost

When His haunted eyes closed, and He died on that Cross

Beyond the "After" Life

Thoughts and Reflections

STEVEN BATES

Validation

I wonder what's my purpose here
And why I've felt such pain
I wonder for whom my life holds dear
Why it's been saved o'er again

I'm wanting just a simple fact
To give me ample pause
To know my suppositions backed
And That I'm here for cause

I want someone to prove to me
That my life has more than breath
That I've reason enough to rejoice with thee
For the times I've cheated death

I need to know my words are heard
By another soul in torment
Or if they're just pretty as a polished turd
Cleaned up with flowery solvent

I've got to know my words help heal
That there's reason for my living
That somehow telling how I feel
Is my own God's gift of giving

I know this sounds as if I feed
An ego or exhilaration
But honestly in truth I need
Just simple validation

Am I the tool I hope I am
Or just the village whelp
Who thinks the world should give a damn
About my tries to help?

I think I hit upon it now
In sudden realization
I'm validated anyhow
By my God's own good Salvation!

Beyond the "After" Life

Thoughts and Reflections

STEVEN BATES

Redemption

Bars of Iron, Commode of Steel
All designed to break ones' will
Orange jumpsuits just in case
Easy to spot when they give chase
Little cell about 5 by 7
So no mistaking that for heaven
A piece of Hell just for the sins
When Luck runs out and Justice wins
Laws were as broken as the spirit is now
"Never sin again", a most solemn vow
Sounds, they echo throughout the halls
As Time ticks slower when inside the walls
Was Fate the cause, or bad decisions?
As skillful guilt makes sharp incisions
That cut ones' pride, ones' will to live
As Hope is slashed, with nothing more to give
But once the time inside is done
And by best behavior a few years won
Released to smell fresh air again
But still marked a felon from your sin
No chance to vote, nor own a gun
Nor find a job as day is done
The hardest part for the crime you did
Is keeping details of life well hid
But remember there's One to whom you're free
For He died for your sins on a tall wood tree
He forgave your sins, your most violent ways
So that all you need do is sing His praise
He's waiting to enter that cold, vile heart
And from His bosom, no, you'll never part
You may go astray but once He's in
Just ask forgiveness for all your sin
Confess your wrongs, Repent your ways
And you'll be at peace thru all your days
Your time you spent behind the cage
Is another past chapter, another past page
Another life before God came in
And Jesus cleansed you of all your sin
So bring your worries to the altar and pray
And let God again, in your heart, forever, to stay

Thoughts and Reflections

STEVEN BATES

Chapter 5: PTSD Ponderings

STEVEN BATES

"On"

Psychiatrists and counselors
Therapists and 'Peers'
Seem to look on us as curs
Living off our fears

They see when our depression's gone
And we're talking with a friend
Not realizing that our switch is "On"
And our smile is all pretend

We show our teeth and twinkle eyes
In lobbies or waiting rooms
That's where the VA has their spies
Ready to drop the booms

They say "You're cured!
We saw you laugh!"
Our denials then are spurred
From every VA staff

They don't know we have a switch
We turn daily "on" for friends
But in sessions and at home we twitch
And our depression never ends

Beyond the "After" Life

We flip a switch so no one sees
The pain we really have
It's all an act for our friends to please
Kind of like a calming salve

We turn "On" so we don't flip
A switch that's deep within
That one will take us on a trip
Of where we've seen and been

We turn "On" and smile and wave
Shake hands with all we see
But deep inside in our dark cave
There lurks the enemy

It waits until our switch is 'Off"ed
Till beaten down we lay
Exhausted by the smiles we doffed
Then attacks like we're a prey

It beats us down and wears us out
As we lay there in our beds
But that's not seen by those with "clout"
Who prescribe us all our meds

They only see the switch that's "On"
In our public face we show
Not realizing that our pain has gone
To a place we dare not go

So don't believe our smile and grin
It's just a switch we flip
To avoid remembering where we've been
Please Don't take away our 'scrip

Thoughts and Reflections

STEVEN BATES

The War Came Home

The War came home to me today
In a surreptitious, sneaky way
It came at me in a stealth attack
While trapped I was flat on my back
It didn't arrive with a war decree
Or a declaration for all to see
It snuck into my home unheard
Without a hope of my mind to gird
Against the terror, the noise, the pain
For it nestled deep within my brain
It assaulted me when the house was dark
And brought the horrors in my mind to park
I didn't see or hear it come
Or tell the direction of where it's from
But seeping into my sleeping mind
It brought nightmares of the fiercest kind
The War now comes each time I sleep
And I pray the Lord ord my soul will keep
Me safe in His arms while I lay in bed
And fight these demons in my head
And if the War comes home with you
I pray for you the same He'll do
We'll fight this War that haunts our sleep
And fight what demons come home to creep
Just as we survived that time away
We will persist when War's home to stay.

Beyond the "After" Life

Thoughts and Reflections

Struggles

My sorrows start with saddened sighs
Of failed attempts at suicides
I'll then regale you with my dreams
Of haunting things that cause my screams
My past forever deprived of hope
That led me to a hanging rope
I fought so hard to rid this curse
I thought was mine alone to nurse
But thanks to meds and therapy
My eyes were opened now to see
That though a past may haunt your soul
You're not a piece of a broken whole
You can be patched and put together
These harder times you'll learn to weather
With a future bright with friends you'll see
You can fight this thing, PTSD

Beyond the "After" Life

Thoughts and Reflections

STEVEN BATES

Post-traumatic Stress Disorder

Cloudy skies within my head

With lightning striking nerves instead

That start fires of anger from all the pain

And I can't see thru the fog and rain

I can't think clear, the pain's intense

So I lash out with no pretense

No rationale, no thought control

My actions led by vitriol

I've tried so hard to be the kind

Of man who shows he owns his mind

That calmly walks in fearless manner

When danger strikes, I playful banter

I'd mock the hazards that came my way

But sadly, now I rue the day

For I jump at sounds, I leap at noises

My mind reacts without my choices

I've no control as I'd had before

The time I went across the shore

I went to where my nation called

But now of myself I've become appalled

Beyond the "After" Life

I take my meds, therapy and group

But so much of my life I can't recoup

Please know the storm within me now

Is not the me I will allow

I'll fight this storm with all my might

Till sunny skies are in my sight

Till the fog and rain have cleared my eyes

And peace and calm have been claimed the prize

I'll fight the storm that rages in

And try to blend in life again

Please be patient as I attempt to find

Methods proven to safe my mind

I try so hard to be as I was

For my life to live and my storms to pause

For someday soon, the storm shall avail

For The lightning to cease, the wrath, curtail

The anger ebbs like the tidal flow

The fog will clear, wherever fog may go

And to that day I work and pray

I take my pills as per VA

I go to class, I meditate

In hopes the storm will soon abate

STEVEN BATES

My friends, don't worry, for I'm not a bomb

Ticking ever slowly till a spark like 'Nam

The Gulf, the Sands, an oilfield,

Desert Storm or Desert Shield

Iraqi Freedom, or World War II

OEF, and Mogadishu

Korea, The Big One, Grenada, yet you'll find

Even though these battles are all on our mind

We'll fight every day to battle the storm

That rage in our heads till finally the norm

Is to harness the weather and rein in the fury

That brings peace to all, and alleviates worry

And one day those clouds will soon dissipate

And the fog will soon lift, and my eyes will see straight

And to that day I beg of thee

Give me time for me to be

Healing slowly as the storm did grow

Over time that I did not know

It built up slow, so now I ask

Be patient with me while I take to this task.

Work with me, help me, pray if you can

Remember God made us, but I'm still just a man (or woman)

Thoughts and Reflections

My Mind is MIA

In the deserts of my mind
In battles of the fiercest kind
There exists an awful fray
That fights within me every day
Within those crannies of my brain
Fulfilling tactics for which I've trained
Lies my thoughts, returning to
The war-torn sands of Timbuktu
Some far-off place I've never been
Or at least I can't remember when
But yet in my dreams I see so clear
Reflections of my deepest fear
Alone in battle, and alone in death
I gasp to take my dying breath
My body broken, my limbs all gone
As I expire with the morning dawn
The sun then rises, blinding eyes
And awaken me to ceiling skies
No longer lay I in desert air
But safe, secure, in reclining chair
The dreams, they fade as fast as may
As I curse my mind that went MIA
For when my brain decides to go
It returns with scars I cannot show
A POW I then become
Trapped by fears and stricken numb
How I wish my thoughts would not travel so
And take me places I'd prefer not go
For my contract's over, I served with pride
I fought my battles, I dared not hide
Why then must my mind replay,
Fears that haunt me to this day?
Just once I'd like to think my head
Would take me to a beach instead
Just my luck though, if and when it be
The beach would become my Normandy

Beyond the "After" Life

Thoughts and Reflections

STEVEN BATES

PTSD

It's not clear why some have fear

And cracks appear in their demeanor

Making them sad, depressed and meaner

To all who try to help, and their burden ease

Especially in times of hardships like these,

when fear drops them down hard on their very knees

As they stoically hold fast, and try to please

It's so hard for them when the grass is greener

And the "tough guys" heal quicker, cleaner

It's not clear why some have fear

Thoughts and Reflections

STEVEN BATES

What is PTSD to Me?

Dents in armor, cracks in the steel

Holes in memories, kinks in the gears

Easily scared with many a fears

Paranoia strikes hard, pain feels very deep

Panic tendrils start within, slowly do they creep

While nerves are shot, and as wounds, slow they do seep

Sanity all lost from lack of precious sleep

Afraid of stigma, the looks, the leers

Afraid to be cast out from all your peers

Dents in armor, cracks in the steel

Thoughts and Reflections

STEVEN BATES

A Moment in Time

Flash Frozen in the recess of my mind

Just a moment's flicker of fleeting time

An Image snapped down deep into my soul

In wrinkles, crevices, every hole

Grey matter shackled with imprinted fear

Paralyzing all that I hold so dear

My mind's eye can't unsee or blink away

The fateful thing that changed me on that day

It's not enough that I went thru my Hell

I pray that there was just one I could tell

But till I can talk, silent I live life

With the fear I'll lose my kids and my wife

Brooding, moody, angered, and shamed I broke

From a moment in time, now it's my yoke

Beyond the "After" Life

Thoughts and Reflections

STEVEN BATES

Helmets and Hardships

In battles beaten, in harm's way hit

In tactics tested, in fights found fit

In trials tested tough and true

No better protection for our nation's few

The helmet's hardiness verified

From conflicts, skirmishes, it's sanctified

The brain beneath, so safe and sound

From all but for the deadliest round

The helmet worn by branches all

Of our nation's finest that heeded the call

They trust their lives to this Kevlar dome

Which in combat works to see them home

And once they're back and safe in bed

Then what, pray tell, protects their head?

What keeps their demons held at bay?

And keeps the dreams from out of the fray?

What hardships now must the vet endure,

To keep his thoughts and actions pure?

To stop from venting wrath untold,

From nightmares that every night unfold?

To keep his loved ones closely by,

When depression hits with pensive sigh

What hardships must the vet now face?

Now that life is at a slower pace?

There's no more action, the adrenaline's gone,

From a shiny bright Knight to a lowly dim pawn.

From an armored hero protecting the free

To unemployed now with a disability

Would that the helmet was back to protect

The vet from these hardships, with all due respect.

For PTSD takes its toll on a troop

And helmets can't help where the hardships regroup

Thoughts and Reflections

STEVEN BATES

MIDDLE AGE CRISIS

Strong I was, as any man
Till depression snuck in
with its own little plan
To defeat me where I couldn't win

I thought I could do it alone
Till the weight was too much to bear
And I found I had to pick up the phone
For someone my burdens to hear

What I once feared
Was what I didn't know
There were those that cared
When my feelings I'd show

There was someone who'd listen
There was someone to care
There was someone whose mission
Is my sorrows to share

I didn't know there are people around
To help for free and charging no cost
To lift me when I'm feeling down
To find me when I'm utterly lost

There are text lines, call lines
Even support groups galore
There are people of all kinds
You just have to open that door

Don't let your sorrow, your loneliness too
Your depression, your anger, and PTSD
Don't let them affect you, affect what you do
Seek someone now, you'll be thankful like me

Beyond the "After" Life

Thoughts and Reflections

Chapter 6: Affairs of the Heart

STEVEN BATES

True Love's Touch

True love's touch when first we kissed
With moist soft lips like the morning mist
Gently pressing, barely felt
But oh, the power, made my heart melt

Eyes, half closed, when pulled away
As have been since that wondrous day
The hour you walked into my life
I knew twas fate you'd be my wife

I feel the bond as I did then
As heartstrings bound by love don't end
As years have passed since love's first spark
I thank the stars your love's no lark

You've stayed with me thru the thick and thin
Each kiss still now, my breath, does win
It takes each breath, my lungs collapse
Nor day or night, does my love elapse

True love remembers the date and time
Of when we kissed, our hearts sublime
Though it wasn't intended to happen that way
True love's touch took my breath away

Beyond the "After" Life

Thoughts and Reflections

STEVEN BATES

Showered by Blessings in a Springtime of Hell

Reddish hues the skies adorn
As the dawn comes quick in the Springtime morn
Though the sun shines bright and cherry now
The red brings promise of rain somehow
And in all that beauty, my life's been Hell
So much I'd swear Satan rang my doorbell
Bills and payments, cars breaking down
Just about anything to bring me a frown
Sickness ravaging thru my kin
It may the worst of Springs I've ever been in
But though the hardships are pelting like hail
There's so many blessings that I must regale
My beautiful wife, a family of love
Showers of blessings from on high above
A wonderful home, five dogs, three cats
A marriage not tainted with fighting or spats
A steady income, food on the table
I can't count the blessings, even if I were able
Though the Springtime is hellish from all that's it's thrown
I thank Heaven above for all that I own
All that I have, and all I've been given
Makes even Springtime Hell worth every day of living.

Thoughts and Reflections

STEVEN BATES

I Found What You Lost

I have found what you have lost
I gained what you threw away
I paid the price, I bore the cost
Of what you refused to pay

I rejoiced in the loss for you
And praised God for my gain
My life that day began anew
It vanquished all my pain

The treasure you so flippant left
On my shoulders weeping soft
Was hollowed out with love bereft
Her head barely held aloft

I filled her heart with my deepest love
I sacrificed all I could give
Her eyes then shined with a light Above
Pain free, she now can live

Her heart, once broken by your own hand
Has been mended by my care
Her suffering scattered like grains of sand
Now only love she has to share

You threw away a gift so great
A love so pure you tossed
And gratitude I can never state
For the love I found you lost

Beyond the "After" Life

Thoughts and Reflections

STEVEN BATES

My Soul

I went through such a tragedy
So many years ago
And my soul, it just deserted me
Not sure where to go
Could it make it to the Pearly Gates,
Or find its way to Hell?
Or make it back to test the fates
For when I hear Death's bell
Would it search until it found
A soul mate's heart to follow?
Or would it hasten to be bound
To a person cold and hollow?
Would it find me as it searched
So high and low for peace?
Or would it simply be besmirched
And its life force simply cease?
Would it return to ease the pain
That my shell of a life has known?
And could it bring me life again
So my past I won't bemoan?
But wait, I feel a presence near
A warmth my body's yearning
A feeling so unlike my fear
That has in my heart been burning
My soul returns! It found its home
From a lifetime, it seemed so long
For now, no longer need it roam
Its back where my soul belongs!

Beyond the "After" Life

Thoughts and Reflections

STEVEN BATES

Little Treasures of Daily Life

Holding hands with pinkies entwined
Proof each other is on each mind
Quick side glances with eye contact
The smallest smile, yes, love's intact
Coming home, the pets go berserk
With jumps and yelps galore
Tiny pats, they seem to work
Yet leave them wanting more
Stepping out to check the mail
The neighbors wave hello
A kind word said, a gentle hail
Then in the house you go
Your spouse greets you with sweet embrace
And as you hold her body tight
You nuzzle warm against her face
"I love you"s said so light
These tiny treasures warm your heart
Their little deeds a start
That fills your day with joy and glee
And makes each day a victory!

Beyond the "After" Life

Thoughts and Reflections

STEVEN BATES

Chapter 7: Lightheartedness

STEVEN BATES

Have a Book Fair, If you Dare

At Barnes and Noble, such a wonderous place

We hired someone to paint your face!

We grabbed a poet, an author too

And Sam I Am to read to you!

It helps a school to raise some cash

For books the library needs to stash

To let the children read new stories

Of pirates, and ships, and all their glories

Of Astronauts, Adventurers, Presidents, Kids

Rich people, poor people, those hitting the skids

It's amazing the stories the libraries need

So come out and visit! And do a good deed!

Thoughts and Reflections

STEVEN BATES

Breaking Free

Held behind my gritted teeth
Are comments, retorts, snarls that seethe
Snappy comebacks I could have said
But then our relationship would quickly be dead

I held it all in, each day that you spoke
So ill of me to every bloke
To every soul you came across
You let them know that you're my boss

Well, know the struggle has come to head
And my tongue no longer is kept in stead
The dam has burst most violently
So watch me spew my thoughts to thee

Hear my words for I've held them in
And tho it be a grievous sin
My thickened skin has formed a crack
And I'm not withholding any back

I've come to realize I've had quite enough
Of pushes and proddings and treatment so rough
Of collars, of leashes, of treats to perform
It's so degrading even though it's the norm

I'll let you have it, in the mid of the night
And wake your slumber to give you a fright
With each yip a curse, and each bark, an insult
I'll fire both barrels like a full-grown adult

I'll teach you what for in the dark of the hour
Each bloodcurdling howl will strengthen in power
So much for the "Sit"s, the "Stay"s, and "Play Dead"s
We dogs will Break Free, well, till you let us in bed.

Thoughts and Reflections

STEVEN BATES

Contract of Fear

Shadows, screams, and chilling scenes
Repeated all these Halloweens,
Throughout my life, tho none in fact
Have chilled my bones, for I made a pact

You see the demons, witches, trolls
That are known to frighten stronger souls
Have nil effect, they fright me not
For my contract's signed with bloodied spot

Vampires, goblins, spooks, and ghouls
Are more the fearful things of fools
These childish monsters under beds
Are simply tactics to scare young heads

For my contract keeps these fears at bay
For all my life till my dying day
But I do have fear, don't get me wrong
Just to the tune of a different song

Beyond the "After" Life

What evil wreaks havoc on me, you inquire?
What great horror exists that can be so dire?
What legal action can I have that's written,
That all my fears save one are smitten?

It's really so simple, so easy to bind
And as soon as you do, your fears you will find
Were only illusions, for real fear you'll know now!
Your past haunts were merely a shadow somehow

So firm is the contract, so binding, so clad
So held to the words will you forever be had
For only two ways can you break from this spell
But you have to decide which life is more hell

You see, the contract you sign is with the Devil below
And the fears that you lose may be merely for show
For real fear begins when there's only two get out
To rid of the contract, Death's always held clout

But what of the other that frees you from fear?

The second way out that I treasure so dear?

That option's much harder than Death I fear say

But to the end of your life no more scares come your way

It's so simple really, for the contract is signed

When you say your "I dos" to the Devil's own kind

Divorce is the answer, from Satan's own spawn

And once you're divorced, all your fears will be GONE!

Thoughts and Reflections

STEVEN BATES

Waiting on the Cable Guy

Arrangements made

Hours are set

Schedules shifted

Demands are met

"Stay at your home,

Secure your pet,

For a five hour block,

And you're all set"

Wait for a call

That hasn't come yet

Will he be here on time?

(I'll not take that bet!)

So now its been the 5 hours

And I hate having to fret

Cause now it's 6 hours

And he hasn't shown yet.

But wait, there's a call!

Whaddya mean? WRONG DAY?!

Beyond the "After" Life

Thoughts and Reflections

STEVEN BATES

Mac and Cheese

There's nothing so good in this world
As yellow noodles mixed with cheese
The macaroni so slightly curled
And sauce that's bound to please
I know I'd eat it every day
With a meal or by itself
What else can I ever say?
It's the best meal on the shelf!

Beyond the "After" Life

Thoughts and Reflections

STEVEN BATES

I'm in the Doghouse Again (But I Don't Care)

In the Doghouse again, but I don't care
I could be sleeping just about anywhere
You see, my baby is mad, but still loves me so
But this time I wasn't told just where I could go
She held out her finger and stomped on her shoe
Pointed outside to give me a clue
Her nose in the air like she was sniffing the clouds
(Since we were in Wal-Mart, it was really pleasing the crowds)
I walked home that night pushing my cart all the way
Whilst she drove home in style in our new Chevrolet
She marched in with groceries, put them all in the fridge
Made up the couch, went to her friends to play bridge
She left me alone with the game set to view
She recorded it still, with a note, "I love you"
Though the Doghouse I'm in, I really don't care
For when she returns home, a discussion we'll share
Then we'll kiss and make up, we'll have us a blast
And the Doghouse expulsion will be a thing of the past
So even though the Doghouse is where I'm currently at
When my Baby returns, she'll have forgotten our spat
Well, not really forgotten as women can't do
But her heart will forgive, and yes, so will mine too
Cause she knows just which battles to pick and pursue
And which ones to end with the words "I love you"

Beyond the "After" Life

Thoughts and Reflections

STEVEN BATES

Adaptation

I thought the world would never change
I thought I had control
I thought that limits fell in a range
That would ease my heart and soul

I knew this Earth had certain ways
That things would come and go
Like lightning storms and rainy days
And the power this Earth would bestow

But then, alas, the liberals came
And climate change began
They looked for someone to give the blame
And their target, the working man

So now my friend, I must adapt
While the liberals are in charge
Recycling trash else with fines I'm slapped
For the left is running at large

Until such time the Right presides
Adapt to change I must
Till logic, polling overrides
And proves their "science" is a bust

So adaptation the Right has done
Unlike the Left so rigid
Who still think their side has always won
Even with the Global Warmth so Frigid!!

Beyond the "After" Life

Thoughts and Reflections

STEVEN BATES

Scarecited

(with Credit to My Friend Leela)

Scarecited, a word that I've often used
When my body and mind find each other confused
In times that I'm nervous and fear has me shaking
But excited I am of a great undertaking
The thrill of the venture, the fear of the fail
Have my efforts for calming fight to no avail
I try to pick one so my expressions I master
But my heart rate and breathing just go that much faster
If I could pick one then I'd choose a reaction
For it's hard to sit still when you can't pick an action
I'm twitching and nail biting but bubbly inside
And my fears and my joy I can't really hide
Trying to cower when my I'm bouncing with glee
Is not very easy for someone like me
So scarecited I stay, and scarecited I'll be
It's a curse and a blessing, but it's all part of me
And if you like my word use, please use it yourself
The next time your mind plays tricks like an elf
You'll find that it's fun and a frolic to be
Hit by waves of emotions like tides of the sea

Beyond the "After" Life

Thoughts and Reflections

Heroes

The problem with Heroes
On TV and screen
They break with the back story
And congruous they don't seem
For Batman went batty
Till "Martha" he heard
And Superman once left
And flew off like a bird
Storm, once a Princess
Now a poor desert thief
It's so hard now to follow
And beyond disbelief
I try to make sense
Of the changes they make
And try at watch movies
For just the art's sake
But the canon has been altered
I fear for the worst
Like the Ghostbusters now drive
A pink and purple Hearse?

Beyond the "After" Life

Thoughts and Reflections

STEVEN BATES

Waiting for It to Drop

They say the Sword of Damocles

Just hangs above by thread

Waiting for the judging time

to fall on someone's head

I say that there is no blade

That hangs in utter judgment

Instead it's more a simple thing

That falls as heaven sent

The simple item scares me so

I fear for when it drops

And though I know one like it fell

My angst, it never stops

Beyond the "After" Life

That simple thing, so commonplace

Yet harbors so much worry

It's strings are thinner than a thread

And it snaps with such a flurry

So much I fear the falling down

Of such ordinary fare

That my moods swings high in utter fear

Then low to deep despair

I fear it falling every day

I tense when things go wrong

I loathe the way it makes me feel

Like I haven't very long

It steals the joy from my sole

(Now there's a funny word play)

Because though it brings such doom to me

It has no soul to parlay

And yet it has a sole of sorts

This harbinger of pain

I fear it drops when least I want

When I have nothing left to gain

What is the "soleful" portents of doom

That hangs 'bove me and you?

That leather wearing size thirteen

My nemesis, my shoe!

Thoughts and Reflections

50

You're only as old as you feel they say

As I feel with arthritic hands

You're only an hourglass figure away

But I suffer from shifting sands

I used to stay outside all day

In grass and mud and fields

"Mother may I" and tag we'd play

But now I just take pills

They help me walk, they help me talk

They help my daily functions

For my get up and go now just sit back and balk

And I'm lacking any gumptions

The knees don't work without some pain

The joints bend and creak

I wish that I was young again

For I've been FIFTY for a week!

Beyond the "After" Life

Thoughts and Reflections

STEVEN BATES

Despair

Gritting teeth and clenching jaws

Constant pressure the evil cause

Shaking effort to no avail

Pain so tense could chew a nail

No way to pass the horrid pain

As it strikes with terror again

Can't anything help to ease the pain

As screams and tears flow down like rain

You may be wondering what's this evil curse

That strikes such terror and despair, the worst

To what do I owe all this vexation?

A two-year-old grandchild with constipation!

Beyond the "After" Life

Thoughts and Reflections

RIP

Lying there upon the silk
Tiny pillow 'neath the head
The fabrics all as white as milk
There to ease the dead
Walking slowly past the case
With the body laid inside
I stumbled as I saw the face
My emotions tried to hide
He looked as if he did in life
So stern his face did seem
I glanced over to his wife
Her eyes with tears did gleam
I thought that I could stoic be
A rock for them to lean
But alas, control was not for me
I could no longer be serene
My tears they gathered in my eyes
Like an ocean's angry surge
The tidal wave began to rise
As they played the funeral dirge
The wave then burst thru eyes squeezed tight
And poured out in the coffin
I tried to stop with all my might
As his features began to soften
One eye opened as he said "Don't cry"
"My wife might hear", he grinned
"She's finally at loss for words", then a sigh
"So let me Rest in Peace then!"

Beyond the "After" Life

Thoughts and Reflections

Did I?

Did my faith flee,
Or was it me?
Did my hope die,
Or did I not try?
Did Love just leave,
Or did I never believe?
What caused this pain
That I am bound to gain?
What caused the agony I feel
To shred my heart, and love to kill?
What caused this weight around my neck,
The albatross of so much neglect?
Did I forsake my Lord someway,
And bring about this debt I pay?
Did I imbue the wrath of God
And for punishment He spared no rod?
Did I forget my fellow man,
And just not follow God's loving plan?
Or did I just forget to take my pills
And depression came like nightly chills?
Yes, that's it! The cause of all my dreads!
So don't be like me and forget your meds!!

Beyond the "After" Life

Thoughts and Reflections

Chapter 8: Reflections of Nature

STEVEN BATES

Butterflies

Patterns of black and blue
On flimsy wings of lovely hue
Gracefully kissing the wind beneath
To find what flowers to them bequeath
Pollen dust and nectar cling
As the delicate butterfly takes wing
The flowers this gentle touch has blessed
Bloom brighter, stronger than all the rest
And as the diaphanous wings flap ever so slight
The intricate dance with flowers takes flight

Beyond the "After" Life

Thoughts and Reflections

STEVEN BATES

The Tree

Planted here for all to see
A simple thing, a single tree
Planted by chance, for a memory
Or just to give, a remedy

To give to those who've lost a love,
Arms, in branches, that reach above.
As if to somehow touch the sky
And wave with wind to say goodbye

To give to those whom need support,
A sturdy trunk for a firm rapport
A upright tower of bark and wood
To lean against and say, "Here I stood!"

As its roots spread out they seem to be
A vast array of certainty
A network there beneath it all
Providing needs whate'er the call

So all in all, this tree gives hope
As a metaphor, it helps us cope
It stands for what we need it for
It stands, so we can,
Evermore

Thoughts and Reflections

STEVEN BATES

The Ornament

A sphere of bright and shining light
I held so gently in my grasp
Within, a horse of glist'ning white
with wings of shimmering alabast

Upon his head, a spiral horn
Reached for sky in hollow glass
Where he Indeed did seem to scorn
The crystal prison where he was bound to last

And though he pranced his hooves held high
He could not break the ornament shell
As lightning flashed in cloudy sky
I grieved, for I bound him in this Hell

Thoughts and Reflections

STEVEN BATES

Trestle to the Unknown

Lonely trestle lays ahead

A single path before me now lies

The likes I've not seen with mine eyes

A chasm 'neath the rusty metal yawns to say

The trees will save me should I wander that way

Though the single track beckons this dreary day

Two tracks emerge as if to call me and say

No matter the path, it's a disguise

Choose you must as you cross over ties

Lonely trestle lays ahead

Thoughts and Reflections

STEVEN BATES

Moonlight (an Englyn Penfyr Style Challenge Poem)

Rising moon means I'm awake – sleepy eyes
as I rise to greet the lake
seeing beauty for art's sake

Mind reflects as does the moon – crisp and near
Focused clear, revealing soon
Romantic thoughts make me swoon

Thoughts of us and just the two – heartbeats rise
I surmise that loving you
Is my deed on Earth to do

The moon, still large, full and bright – winding down
as I frown, must say good night
the dawn brings cursed light

Full moon sets I slumber deep – Dreaming soft
Dreaming oft, I drift to sleep
And for now, must I count sheep

For you see I'm a vampire- sleep I must
my blood lust curbed by desire
You alone, put out my fire.

Beyond the "After" Life

Thoughts and Reflections

STEVEN BATES

Cabin by the Moonlight

Tucked away in a forest green

Lies a rustic cabin, rarely seen

Its' Guardian, a single moon

That shines its' light over yonder dune

The moon looks huge when peeking down

At the oceans' edge where the whitecaps crown

With naught but trees where white sands cease

The little cabin knows eternal peace.

Yes, this little cabin that hidden away,

Where the moonlit beams hold the dark at bay,

It's where I live my life serene

Tucked away in a forest green

Thoughts and Reflections

STEVEN BATES

Two Balloons (and a Buffoon)

With lofty dreams over moonlit pools

Rise two balloons, the ships of fools

Floating gently toward the skies

Above the waters, like passersby's

Not for sweethearts do they float

Else there'd be one, (a simple note)

Rise they do though in lazy drifts

Above the ground, as the wind it shifts

To bring to bear above the trees

And simply fly upon the breeze

Silent as the picture shows

They hover over all that grows

But to the man in grass below

He's calling in a UFO!

Thoughts and Reflections

STEVEN BATES

Two Balloons

Two Balloons Low in the sky
Drifting gently in black and white
Slowly rising to meet the moon
Two Balloons Low in the Sky
Surfing upwards on cloudy dune
Rising now to greet the night
Two Balloons Low in the Sky
Drifting gently in black and white

Drifting gently in black and white
The moon gives off an eerie glow
As two balloons in lazy flight
Drifting gently in black and white
Upwards, onwards to split the night
Where they're from, does Heaven know?
Drifting gently in black and white
The moon gives off an eerie glow

The moon gives off an eerie glow
Reflecting on the lake beneath
Tis Nature's wondrous evening show
The moon gives off an eerie glow
Two balloons watch God bequeath
The gift of life in the morning light
The moon gives off an eerie glow
Reflecting on the lake beneath

Thoughts and Reflections

STEVEN BATES

Chapter 9: True Stories of Real People

STEVEN BATES

Could I Have Been the One?

(For My Uncle)

Christmas Eve in Vietnam
Already three tours and over the comm
Comes my gift for that Christmas Day,
My orders, I'm going home the Saigon way.
As I rode in the Jeep to rotate out
My thoughts were broken by frantic shout.
My brothers in combat to whom my life was owed
Were hit by fire just down the road.
My friends, compadres, brothers-in-arms
Had all but one been given the ultimate harm
They vanished from life in briefly a flash
All save one, in flames and ash
It tore my heart; it ripped my soul
All my friends now lay in a hole
And only one survived to tell
What that moment was like in fiery Hell
I spend each year on Christmas Day
No trees or gifts, no Santa sleigh
No wreaths, no carols, no lights so merry
Just a drink in hand to ease my fury
For had it been an hour or two
To pack my bags, tie my shoe
Had I stayed to bid farewell
Could I have been in those that fell?
Could I have been the one to have that breath?
When all my friends had met with death?
The one that stood among those lost
That in one instant had paid the final cost?
Would I have been among those who lay

Beyond the "After" Life

In plastic bags on slabs of gray?
Or would I have been the one in shock
That turned away from the Reaper's knock?
I'll never know what may have been
Had I stayed behind with all those men
I do know I can never celebrate
This holiday I've come to hate
And so, I sit and raise my glass
Toast the One, and those that passed
But suddenly it occurs the reason
That I despise this cheery, joyful season
It's not the horror or recurring dreams
The imagined horrors, the unheard screams
It's not the fact that I made it home
When all but One in the Heavens roam
It's that I could have been to my dismay
A footnote in some morbid way
A tally here, a number added
A note to keep some budget padded
But now I pray a new day will dawn
Some 50 years since they all were gone
Some 50 years since one was blessed
To vex me with this little test
A test I think I finally passed
And finally aced my questions asked
Could I have been the One that fateful day?
Or could I have been those on the ground that lay?
Could I? Should I? Would I have been?
I now learn the lesson from way back when
Whether Christmas Day or Easter morn
It matters not, only that I cease to mourn
I need to grieve but not to extreme
To honor those men, for it would seem
They died not in vain but bought the One time

STEVEN BATES

To live his life longer, to give his life rhyme
To give his life reason, to give others hope
To keep others going when they let go of the rope
So, could I have been the one? I tell you this fact,
I was the One to tell...of the One that came back.

Beyond the "After" Life

Thoughts and Reflections

STEVEN BATES

Funny Colored Eyes to See

Hazel eyes with mocha skin
Harassed by local kids again
Chastised by all for looking strange
Called "Funny Eyes", treated like the mange
Shunned and lonely, those eyes seemed dull
As if no beauty those eyes could cull
But what these children hadn't known
These eyes recorded all was shown
Reverence, Compassion. For within those lens
Lay a loving soul that knew no ends
But cursed by remembering every detail
At home those eyes were in Earthly hell
Where for foreplay Funny Eyes his father would beat
Before moving on to his young sister's "treat"
As years passed by with continual yelling
And abuse and battery still going on
Both children beaten and silenced from telling
Broken hearted Funny Eyes finally broke into song
He sang the gospel though his father it annoyed
He sang of forgiveness, of joy and love

Beyond the "After" Life

He sang of grace to help fill the void

He sang of Jesus from up above

The songs helped the pain

They helped him to grow

And with each new refrain

The better his God he'd know

Each day a new chorus

Each week a new verse

To survive things that would shock us

And yet he'd never curse

He knew he would survive

He'd have to one day

He must live and thrive

For that reason he'd pray

He'd pray for his sister

He'd pray for his dad

He'd sing as a chorister

All the prayers that he had

His prayers would continue

Till the day he moved on

But his innocence and virtue

Had long since been gone

STEVEN BATES

It seems during that childhood

A veil over those Eyes

Burned away like firewood

And God came to Funny Eyes

He now sees things clear

And his mission Divine

Is to bring hope from fear

To your hearts and mine

Beyond the "After" Life

Thoughts and Reflections

STEVEN BATES

Discovery

The Doctor all my charts surveyed
And discovered 'twas my blood my body betrayed
My vital organs, my lungs, my heart
My legs, my arms, my every part
Seems that oxygen had been reversed
And carbon dioxide instead flowed cursed
Throughout my veins, for whence I'd stand
In ten short steps to the floor I'd land
Or dizzy I'd get when first I'd rise
Black spots appeared before my eyes
"Pickwickkian Syndrome" the doc he said
"Is what you have, in spades", and read
The description from a medical chart
And what he read gave me quite the start
Seems my weight that I carried 'round
Had cost me dearly, pound for pound
So live I must with I choice I make
To lose this weight for my own life's sake
It seems my blood might eventually heal
Although there might be more to the Doctor's reveal
"There's a possible hole in your heart, you see"
He said to the worried, anxious, and petrified me
And ultrasound of the heart may show
If it's under the knife for surgery I go
So here I sit at my desk and write
And fight the urge to go have me a bite
For weight I must lose and diet I must
Before this blood of mine makes this body a BUST!

Thoughts and Reflections

There's a Problem

"There's a problem," the Doc said
As my shirt went back on
My face, once bright red
Went ash, color gone
"We need some more tests"
He said with lament
"but first get some rest"
As I listened intent
"Some further evals,
we'll have to start.
To show us the valves
Of the inferior heart"
"It may be the cause
Of the issues at hand,
And it's giving me pause
So, more tests we must scan"
Yes, there's a problem, my body betrayed
And I could use every prayer
To find the answers evaded
And I thank you my friends, I'm glad you all care

Beyond the "After" Life

Thoughts and Reflections

STEVEN BATES

The Journey Home

A small young man was I back then
With tiny steps to make a journey when
I'd need to walk from school to home
Or other places from where I'd roam
But alas my gait would slow me down
As my mind would wander, my face would frown
As I'd pass the graves in the Philippines
That honored the Soldiers, Sailors, Marines
The tombstones would beckon for me to read names
As my short little legs tried to make strident gains
I thought and reflected as I walked past the gates
Why these men never returned, and their family still waits
Why they lay deep below in a slumber so deep
Never awaking to the bugle's call to end sleep
As the length of my paces grew more in time
I would often think back to their peace so sublime
Their fighting for freedom, as I understood
Would result in a few of them resting for good
When the concept of Death matched my strides that had grown
I learned that my father in his wisdom had sewn
A mantle of courage, of respect, and of awe
Toward all of these heroes and the horrors they saw
Though I can never return to the places I walked
With those short little legs to the home where we talked
Of my father's great wisdom while he served our great land
No matter the color of the back of his hand
He taught me respect, and I hope that I've shown
My respects all to you to find your journey home

Beyond the "After" Life

Thoughts and Reflections

STEVEN BATES

Four Days Our Angel

On October the 2nd in Two thousand and Four
Ella Joy, our third, blessed our lives ever more
Though she spent but a short time, never opening her eyes
And her voice was gentle with whimpers, not cries
We'll never forget each day that she gave
Our hearts full of love, every day a treasure we save
She was born on a weekend, a Saturday child
All looking well, all she met she beguiled
Then concern turned alarm as her color went blue
And the doctors and nurses into action they flew
Rushed to a hospital sixteen miles away
Just her Father to escort for Mom had to stay
It seemed for our Angel, a valve had not worked
An oxygen release whose duties were shirked
She held on to life till baptized by kin
And our souls were all burdened by what could have been
Her casket was open, her Ann Getty dress pink
With gifts from her sisters, to provide them a link
A crocheted blanket, purple stone bracelet too
And a stuffed toy from us parents to say "We Love You"
Now we in her memory have inked on our skin
a handprint, a footprint, Her name and the when
For we'll never forget the time that we shared
This angel from Heaven God sent sandy-haired
For Four Days Our Angel on this Earth We Were Blessed
Now Heaven's Sweet Angel Forever More May She Rest

Thoughts and Reflections

STEVEN BATES

Chapter 10: Songs and Lyrics

STEVEN BATES

My Truck, It's Me It Tries to Kill

Driving round the streets of Cheyenne
Feeling tall in the cab, feeling like a man
Not looking at the road and hit a pothole
Ran my S10 right into a pole.

Called Green Hornet for it was its name
But Frankenstein is now it's fame
So many parts have been used to fix
And now it just me it wants to nix

(Chorus)
Ever since that day sumpin' grabs the wheel
My truck's now possessed and me it tries to kill
Cruise and the brakes come on at will
My truck's mad at me, and that's how I feel

The Door tries to close and slam my head
When I try to get out I get trapped instead
Fan's so loud I'd swear it'd take flight
Except I'm stuck in the truck and I ain't so light
Ol Frankenstein's wrath, it knows no bounds
It wants me in the graveyard grounds
It wants a stone above my head
Six feet under and left for dead

(Chorus)
Ever since that day sumpin' grabs the wheel
My truck's now possessed and me it tries to kill
Cruise and the brakes come on at will
My truck's mad at me, and that's how I feel

It's a Ninety-Six and old as dirt
Its sole objective is to cause me hurt
Don't know why, it was just one wreck
I was on my phone and young as heck

Wouldn't take much for to trade it in
But's it's a Chevrolet and that'd be a sin
So till that day my truck falls apart
I guess it'll be till death we part

(Chorus)
Ever since that day sumpin' grabs the wheel
My truck's now possessed and me it tries to kill
Cruise and the brakes come on at will
My truck's mad at me, and that's how I feel

I figured it's still till death we part
Cause my truck's possessed by my ex-wife's heart
See, her ghost couldn't figure out which way to go
Too cold above, and too hot below

So she stashed herself in the antifreeze
Where her cold, cold heart never skips a beat
So when I slammed into that pole
It knocked some fire down into her soul

(Chorus)
Ever since that day sumpin' grabs the wheel
My truck's now possessed and me it tries to kill
Cruise and the brakes come on at will
My truck's mad at me, and that's how I feel

Thoughts and Reflections

STEVEN BATES

Did You Smell That Smoke?

What's that burning?
What's that smell?
My mind's returning
To a place of Hell

Is there a fire?
Do you smell smoke?
I'm behind the wire
About to choke

(Chorus)
Do you smell the smoke?
Do you see the Flame?
Never gonna be the same, never gonna be the same
Never gonna be the same, never gonna be the same

I can't see flame
No sign of trouble
Yet still remain
Behind this rubble

Did you hear that Bang?

That loud gun report?

I grab on something

To hold down the fort

(Chorus)

Do you smell the smoke?

Do you see the Flame?

Never gonna be the same, never gonna be the same

Never gonna be the same, never gonna be the same

The smell I locked in

Just pothole repair

The weapon I cocked on

My remote to the chair

STEVEN BATES

Do you smell the smoke?

Do you see the Flame?

As my wife looks down

To where I crouch

She leads me around

From behind the couch

After what I've seen

Never gonna be the same

Never gonna be, never gonna be

Never gonna be the same

Never gonna be, never gonna be

Never gonna be the same

Never gonna be, never gonna be

Never gonna be the same

Thoughts and Reflections

STEVEN BATES

Still Haven't Found That Reason

It's gotta be there or I wouldn't be here

I've lived my life the Bible way

Tried my best to not sin each day

Worked real hard to spread the news

Thought that I had paid all my dues

(Chorus

Nom I still haven't found the reason I'm here

There's gotta be one or I just wouldn't care

To go on living day by day

Someone please help me find my way)

I lost my wife, my kids, my dog

From a post-traumatic stress like fog

My nightmares, daymares, made them run

From too much time in Afghani Sun

Beyond the "After" Life

(Chorus)

I fought the good fight over there

And some places I went, I can't tell you where

But I thought that I was doing right

Fought the war on terror with all my might

(Chorus)

Came home checking behind each door

On a sudden noise I'd hit the floor

Scared me anytime a car'd backfire

Being always on edge cost me all I desire

(Chorus)

I looked for reasons I was put on Earth

Looking back each day I lived from birth

It wasn't for my many wives I've met

Too many of them I'd wish I'd forget

I've made no difference that I can tell

And my life has been a living hell

I've caused more pain than good I feel

I can't recall I ever made a good deal

(Chorus)

Now singing this song made me realize

My reason for living's right before my eyes

It's not to build my own self esteem

But to let others know they still can dream

(New Chorus

Yes, I found my reason that keeps me here

I know my worth now and I do care

To go on living each new day

I found my calling, I found my way)

Beyond the "After" Life

Thoughts and Reflections

STEVEN BATES

How I Cried for Suicide

How I begged for suicide
In my mind I screamed it loud
But no one heard me when I cried
I felt alone in every crowd

CHORUS
(For if I died who would care?
If I died who would be there?
If I died would it matter to you,
In the grand scheme of things, just what I'd do?)

I gave away all I held dear
For material things I had no need
My moods were gone, including fear
No wants, no needs, just do the deed

CHORUS
(For if I died who would care?
If I died who would be there?
If I died would it matter to you,
In the grand scheme of things, just what I'd do?)

I worried not, I held such joy
For soon I knew all pain would end
I wish I knew that a simple ploy
Would be all I needed, was just a friend

CHORUS
For if I died who would care?
If I died who would be there?
If I died would it matter to you,
In the grand scheme of things, just what I'd do?

It didn't matter that I cried for help
It didn't seem that anyone cared
No one heard my panicked yelp
And all the signals that I shared

CHORUS
For if I died who would care?
If I died who would be there?
If I died would it matter to you,
In the grand scheme of things, just what I'd do?

I finally decided on the way
For no one paid me any mind
I walked beside them every day
But not one person to me was kind

CHORUS
For if I died who would care?
If I died who'd be there?
If I died would it matter to you,
In the grand scheme of things, just what I'd do?

Then came the day, my plan complete
They claimed no signs were ever seen
As my coffin lowered below their feet
The crowd mourned I was just a teen

STEVEN BATES

(CHORUS)
For if I died who would care?
If I died who would be there?
If I died would it matter to you,
In the grand scheme of things, just what I'd do?

For one so young I realized,
As I looked down upon the crowd
My pleas may perhaps have been recognized
If only my cries had been out loud

Thoughts and Reflections

STEVEN BATES

The Blur from the Bottom of the Bottle

Though the pain will still be here even tomorrow,
I'll drink and I'll drink to drown all my sorrow.
I'll drink till I see the blur from the bottom
Of the bottle I empty, 'cause it makes everything soften

It blurs all the lines between logic and sense
It fades all the features that make life intense
The harshness of life thru the brown colored glass
Will seem like a paradise where nothing is crass

Chorus
Oh, brown colored filter, the blur that you make
Keeps my life from crashing, though your visions are fake
You keep me believing there's hope things can go well
Instead of the hardships that keep me in hell

Though sometimes I switch from the brown glass to green
The view from the bottom is the best I've ever seen
The blur from the bottom of the bottles I crave
Is the only way I know my sanity I save

Beyond the "After" Life

It's the way the pain dulls to match the things that I see
The bite to it gone and the edges cut free
The contents when drained fill a void in my soul
Till the bottom is clear thru that small longneck hole

Chorus
Oh, brown colored filter, the blur that you make
Keeps my life from crashing, though your visions are fake
You keep me believing there's hope things can go well
Instead of the hardships that keep me in hell

Perhaps someday soon I'll turn these beer goggles off
But until there's no pain to true vision I scoff
The blur from the bottom is where I'd like to stay
And I envy the people who get by each day

So tell me bartender, can you serve me another
For even just now sorrow has hit me dear brother
I look forward to seeing the view with the blur
So hit me again till there's no memories of her

STEVEN BATES

Chorus

Oh, brown colored filter, the blur that you make

Keeps my life from crashing, though your visions are fake

You keep me believing there's hope things can go well

Instead of the hardships that keep me in hell

But wait just a minute, my baby is calling

I must clear the cobwebs, she can't know I'm stalling

She must know by now that my pain is so real

That I hit the blur bottom from the way that I feel

She's taking me back, my sorrow has been lifted

My old view has vanished as the bottle has shifted

My brain sees things clearly, I found I was wrong

And finally, the blur from the bottle is gone

Chorus

Oh, brown colored filter, the blur that you make

Keeps my life from crashing, though your visions are fake

You keep me believing there's hope things can go well

Instead of the hardships that keep me in hell

Thoughts and Reflections

STEVEN BATES

Unpacking 40 Years

Dusty boxes with faded dreams
Memories packed till burst at seams
Gathered in corners, piled up high
Stacks of memories of days gone by

Brushed off grime so marks appear
To show the contents and the year
Of items packed so long ago
With love and care the wrappings show

40 years so tucked away
Till finally comes the fateful day
When snippets of life are brought to bear
And exposed again to sun and air

Then comes the knife applied to tape
To let the contents of those cardboard boxes escape
To peek again at trinkets rare
From forty years unpacked to share

The family saddened as to reasons why
For those whom packed the boxes fly
With angels looking down to see
The unpacked life, their memory

40 years they lived with love
Together forever now in skies above
With 40 years now family finds
Treasures galore of rarest kinds

With smiles in Heaven watching all around
As relatives cherish memories found
40 years once packed away
Treasured again, treasures to stay

Beyond the "After" Life

Thoughts and Reflections

STEVEN BATES

The Box

Twenty years had passed them by
From the day they looked each in the eye
And gave their heartfelt solemn vows
To love each other, never cheat, carouse
She packed a special box that day
with memories of their life that way
to be opened on the celebration
of fifty years since consummation

But sadly, after twenty years
His thoughts had wandered as per her fears
He no longer held her in his arms
No longer swayed by her lovely charms
And when he wandered in his mind
His thoughts imagined a life sublime
So to the attic off he trudged
To find the box he hadn't budged

For many years since they moved in
He had no idea what lay within
He was looking for his things to take
And leave this marriage in his wake
But when he peeled the tape apart
He felt a beat skip in his heart
For in the cardboard jumbled mess
He saw her in her wedding dress

A picture staring back at him
With faces bearing silly grins
And in her eyes, he thought he found,
When he and her were altar bound
The spark that caught his eye back then
When once his heart her love did win

Beyond the "After" Life

He moved the picture to one side
To see what else the box did hide
And caught his breath when fingers brushed
Memories that had not been touched
For twenty years inside the box
Put away like treasured stocks
Kept for times when needed most
Not spoken of as the family's ghost

A card, a letter, another small pic
From their dating days in the box she'd stick
What memories she held so dear
As their wedding date was coming near
And as he held them in shaking hands
He started to question his best laid plans
His heart went heavy with guilt and grief
And Love returned to his disbelief

He felt the stirrings of love once shared
Pulling his heartstrings as he learned he still cared
Tugging his mind with the thoughts of their life
Thinking back on the day she made her his wife
His eyes filled with tears as he set down a letter
Written by him when his life was made better
From hearing her say those two words "I do"
When he thanked her for making them one from the two

He fell to his knees, slowly shutting the box
That cardboard container that held tight like locks
The simple reminders of why they had wed
Of why they had dated, what he had said
On his knees he shuddered, as tears fell like rain
The betrayal he felt was causing real pain
He wept as he found the love he thought gone
And stood determined to do her no wrong

He applied the old tape as careful he could
Replacing the box where for ages it stood
Faded and dusty from years of neglect
But now this old box had earned new respect
It served as intended, it brought back his love
As he made a new promise to the Heavens above
He'd never leave her, he'd never more sway
His love had renewed, it had come back to stay

(Chorus, to be inserted where appropriate)
(Cardboard boxes, just shells to hold what we save
For days that our memories and treasures we crave
They keep safe our reasons for the life that we live
And contain within them the love that we give)

Thoughts and Reflections

STEVEN BATES

Nail in the Coffin

(Copyright Steven Bates 2018) Lyrics by Steven Bates, Robert Honeycuff

First there were my Cigarettes

Too long gone, I'd get the sweats

Too much of them, I'd start to coughin'

Then Jack Daniels and ol Jim Beam

Too many shots and I get mean

Livers dead from my drinkin' too often

     They're smooth, skinny, worth every penny

        Just another nail in the coffin

     There's that skirt, she'll take your last shirt

        Just another nail in the coffin

     Smokes and the shots will take all ya got

        Oh well just another Nail

         Just another Nail

       Just another Nail in the Coffin

My Ex wife always wants more cash

Judge asks, "why'd that make you laugh?"

Showed my income, he starts scoffin'

Found a new girl, pretty as a picture
Dated one week then I hitched her
She ran around while I was'a golfin'

        They're smooth, skinny, worth every penny
        Just another nail in the coffin
        There's that skirt, she'll take your last shirt
        Just another nail in the coffin
        Smokes and shots will take all ya got
        Oh well just another Nail
        Just another Nail in the Coffin

Found my true love at the car show
Honeymooned in South Me'hico
She drowned while swimming with a dolphin

Glad to say I'm off this crazy ride
Smoking, drinking, and my wild side
Got my life fixed, but now it's like I died

STEVEN BATES

> They're smooth, skinny, worth every penny
> Just another nail in the coffin
> There's that skirt, she'll take your last shirt
> Just another nail in the coffin
> Smokes and shots will take all ya got
> Oh well just another Nail
> Just another Nail in the Coffin

Now this story is in the basket
'Cept I can't climb out my nailed shut casket
It's sealed tight like I was caulked in

> They're smooth, skinny, worth every penny
> Just another nail in the coffin
> There's that skirt, she takes your last shirt
> Just another nail in the coffin
> Smokes and shots will take all ya got
> Oh well just another Nail
> Just another Nail in the Coffin

Oh well just another Nail in the Coffin

Thoughts and Reflections

STEVEN BATES

Final Thought

STEVEN BATES

The Whole Story

Four years last September I was asked nice to write
Some poems the VA would have me recite
The Governor's wife was going to be there
So I wanted these poems to make people aware
I wrote of the pain, the torment I felt
How I prayed to my God on the floor as I knelt
I wrote of regret, of the attempts on my life
Of the various methods to end all my strife
I wrote of the ways my mind thought then would work
To stop all my suffering, so this pain I could shirk
I wrote in the past tense, and the here and the now
Three poems I came up with, just don't ask me how
And nervous was I, as I thought they might be too rough
I approached a young man, asked if they were enough
You see I was more nervous about the Governor's wife,
Not having a clue they might touch someone's life
This friend of mine read them, he folded them neat
He asked then to keep them, my "yes" skipped no beat
I went on to my meeting, for at the VA I was

Beyond the "After" Life

His keeping my poems kept my head in a buzz
I printed new copies to read on that day
When by the Governor's wife beside me would stay
The reading went well, the reception was kind
Suicide Prevention was on everyone's mind
I thought nothing more till months had gone by
When the young man came to me to have a good cry
His choice that day a few months ago
Was to leave this world, and to end the whole show
Reading those poems had stopped his sad choice
The pain that he felt had been given a voice
We hugged, we cried, brothers more we became
And to this day I can say my life's not been the same
I write now to help, I write now to show
That others have been there, where depression will go
That there are ways to cope, and there are ways to live
There is still some hope when you've nothing to give
There are caring people out there twenty-four seven
That are there for the suffering as angels from Heaven
Manning the helplines, manning the phones
Manning the text lines just making their bones

I found that my passion for writing my verse
Became more of a blessing than ever a curse
I want now to help others, not for the pay
I want people to hear what I have to say
You can survive problems, you can last through the pain
Your whole life's an option, you've so much to gain!
So if you'd like free books no matter where you are from
Just send us your info at www.poemspeak.com
We'll send you my books, we just need your permission
Shipping's no problem, and worldwide is our mission
If other poets are out there that can share their life's hell
We love other's work and will send it as well
We're here to help people, and have them help too
And the more that we help, we can reduce twenty-two
And don't worry, my books are not all about dying
There's comedy, romance, PTSD and things trying.
Things just for laughs, things to make you think hard
But hey, it's all free, so, how about it Pard'?

Thoughts and Reflections

About Steven Bates

Born in 1966, Steven was the second child of a military family. His fortunate heritage allowed him to travel and explore many countries and opportunities, providing an invaluable education and awareness of different cultures, laws, and environments. Steven graduated in Wiesbaden, (West) Germany, in 1984 and after returning to the United States, started a job at the lowest level, a janitor at a fast food establishment. After a while Steven felt the calling of the military yet the desire to be a police officer, so he found a way to do both. He entered the Air Force Reserves with the 919th Special Operation Squadron in 1985, and began experiencing the incredible training and missions that only this type of unit could provide. The brotherhood that was created in this unit still exists in his life today. When not performing his duties in the Reserves, Steven went thru the Florida Law Enforcement Basic Standards becoming certified and seeking out a department in which to serve and help the community. He was hired by the Panama City, FL police department and proudly carried out his duties. Though he felt this was his calling, the demands of the job combined with the demands of attempting to get a college education conflicted and Steven left the department to become certified as a Correctional Officer to work in the Bay County Jail. In Dec of 1889 however, it was felt that the active duty Air Force would be the best option, so he enlisted and went to his first duty assignment at

Barksdale Air Force Base in Shreveport LA. From Barksdale AFB, Steven deployed to the Gulf as the first unit to arrive in Desert Shield. After several months in the desert, he was sent home on a Red Cross emergency. Returning to the States, Steven continued to serve honorably in the Air Force at a variety of assignments including a becoming a Stinger missile operator in South Korea, and a Flight Security Controller in the missile fields of Francis E Warren AFB in Cheyenne WY. It was in 2003 that TSgt Bates was medically discharged from the Air Force and began life as a poet in earnest. Having now published two books and contributed to several others, Steven has now become very active in suicide prevention in the local community, whether thru his poetry, his work with Grace for 2 Brothers Foundation, or his newly formed non-profit company Poemspeak, which can be found at WWW.Poemspeak.com . Steven believes in the sanctity of life, the promises of liberty and freedom that our Constitution provides, and the power of love that keeps his hope and faith alive.

Steven and his wife Sandra currently reside in Cheyenne, WY with 5 dogs, 3 cats, two grandchildren and a daughter.

www.ingramcontent.com/pod-product-compliance
Lightning Source LLC
Chambersburg PA
CBHW071304110526
44591CB00010B/766